DEEP WATER

DEEP WATER

Encountering God's Extraordinary

Grace in Everyday Life

JACKIE McCOWN

DEEP WATER

Encountering God's Extraordinary Grace in Everyday Life

© 2025 Jackie McCown.

All rights reserved. No part of this publication may be reproduced, distributed, or transmitted in any form or by any means, including photocopying, recording, or other electronic or mechanical methods, without the prior written permission of the publisher, except in the case of brief quotations embodied in critical reviews and certain other noncommercial uses permitted by copyright law. For permission requests, please contact the author.

Independently Published by Jacquelynn McCown | Montgomery, Ohio

Printed in the United States of America

ISBN: (Hardback) 978-1-7373703-2-1

ISBN: (Paperback) 978-1-7373703-3-8

ISBN: (EPUB) 978-1-7373703-4-5

Library of Congress Control Number (LCCN): 2025915792

To Contact the Author: JACKIEMCCOWN.COM

For Cheri
Who first led me to the Little Way—
to see holiness in small things,
to choose presence over performance,
and to believe that God meets us most tenderly
in the quiet depths of ordinary life.
Thank you for showing me how to dwell in the deep water.

And for Sue
Who taught me to contend—
to fight with faith for what is good and true,
to press in when the path is unclear,
and to believe that life and health are worth the struggle.
You are a fierce and faithful warrior,
constantly whispering courage to my soul.
Thank you for reminding me to keep
stopping, challenging, and choosing.

SCRIPTURE TRANSLATIONS USED

Scripture quotations marked ESV are taken from The Holy Bible, English Standard Version. ESV® Text Edition: 2016. Copyright © 2001 by Crossway Bibles, a publishing ministry of Good News Publishers.

Scripture quotations marked with the designation GW are taken from GOD'S WORD®. © 1995, 2003, 2013, 2014, 2019, 2020 by God's Word to the Nations Mission Society. Used by permission.

Scripture quotations marked KJV are taken from the King James Bible, which is in the public domain.

Scripture quotations marked NASB are taken from the New American Standard Bible®, Copyright © 1960, 1971, 1977, 1995, 2020 by The Lockman Foundation. All rights reserved.

Scripture quotations marked NCB are taken from the SAINT JOSEPH NEW CATHOLIC BIBLE® Copyright © 2019 by Catholic Book Publishing Corp. Used with permission. All rights reserved."

Scripture quotations marked NIV are taken from the Holy Bible, New International Version®, NIV® Copyright ©1973, 1978, 1984, 2011 by Biblica, Inc.® Used by permission. All rights reserved worldwide.

Scripture quotations marked NKJV are taken from the New King James Version®. Copyright © 1982 by Thomas Nelson. Used by permission. All rights reserved.

*Scripture quotations marked NLT are taken from the **Holy Bible**, New Living Translation, copyright © 1996, 2004, 2015 by Tyndale House Foundation. Used by permission of Tyndale House Publishers, Inc., Carol Stream, Illinois 60188. All rights reserved.*

Scripture quotations marked TPT are from The Passion Translation®. Copyright © 2017, 2018, 2020 by Passion & Fire Ministries, Inc. Used by permission. All rights reserved. ThePassionTranslation.com.

CONTENTS

Introduction 9

CHAPTER 1   *Relationships* 13

CHAPTER 2   *Marriage* 33

CHAPTER 3   *Parenting* 53

CHAPTER 4   *The Character of God* 69

CHAPTER 5   *Faith* 93

CHAPTER 6   *Virtue* 123

CHAPTER 7   *Self Awareness* 145

CHAPTER 8   *Performance* 171

CHAPTER 9   *Adversity* 193

CHAPTER 10   *Authentic Life* 217

CHAPTER 11   *Gaining Perspective* 243

CHAPTER 12   *One Last Thought* 257

Praise for Deep Water 261

About the Author 263

INTRODUCTION

Deep Water (n.)—

The silent sanctuary of the soul where God's presence moves in sacred stillness, clear depths—unshaken, vast, and pure. It surrounds me like a gentle tide, shields me like an unseen hand, and flows through me with a quiet, unwavering divine truth that cleanses, insight that awakens, and peace that settles and restores from within.

Life, in all its beauty and complexity, has a way of unfolding slowly, shaped by the seasons we walk through, the people we love, and the questions we carry.

Most mornings, I begin the day the same way—hands wrapped around a warm mug of coffee, taking a breath before the noise of the day begins. It's a small ritual, but one that makes space for stillness. And in that stillness, something deeper often stirs.

I'm a wife, a mother of three grown sons, a daughter, a friend, and a woman who has spent much of my life on a quiet but steady journey of faith. It's taken me through unexpected places, always reminding me that our lives don't move in straight lines.

Over time, I've come to see that faith isn't a matter of having all the answers or always feeling certain. It's about paying attention. It's about learning to live in the deep water, trusting that even in the messiest or most ordinary moments, something sacred is happening.

Most of my spiritual life has grown in the in-between places: in the chaos of family life, in the quiet of early mornings, and in the simple conversations that open us up to something more. I've come to believe that God often meets us in the quiet, the overlooked, the everyday.

If you've ever wondered whether the sacred could be found in the ordinary or if your life—just as it is—might be a place where something holy is already happening, then this is for you.

So, come. Pull up a chair. Let's sit for a while and soak in the mystery, quiet, unhurried, and surrounded by something deeper. Let's notice the beauty as we are gently drawn into the peace only God can give. Let's rest, weightless from the cares of the world, in waters that know our name.

If you listen, you will catch a glimpse of heaven in the middle of your everyday, a quiet reminder of something your soul has always longed for. Even in the messiness of life, there is a still, steady voice. Let's discover the wonder of faith woven into our everyday lives.

This book is not just a reflection on theology or a roadmap for anyone wrestling with their faith journey or navigating the shadows of doubt. It's an open invitation to witness the divine woven into the fabric of the ordinary—to behold God's quiet work in the small, the simple, and the overlooked. It's about discovering joy tucked inside the mundane and meeting grace where life feels most unsteady.

In deep water, we do not drift—we dwell.

RELATIONSHIPS

Relationships are why we are here. The very foundation of our existence, reflecting God's design for connection with others and with Him. It is in the deep moments of vulnerability, truth, and love that we find our purpose and fulfill our fundamental need for belonging. Whether through friendships, family, or faith, relationships challenge us to grow and remind us of our need for one another. But connection doesn't begin with effort—it begins with presence. In a world driven by doing, the quiet power of simply being—attentive, open, and loving—forms the true heart of relationship.

CONNECTIVITY

It's an almond milk latte in the pretty Poland mug and Saturday morning quietness interrupted by rediscovered clock chimes (and now I know why the batteries haven't been replaced in 15+ years).

Polyvagal theory. Are you familiar? The Mac and I learned about it yesterday, and oh-my-goodness! It is a life changer. This medical theory explains how our autonomic nervous system, particularly the vagus nerve, participates in social engagement and emotional regulation. Ultimately, it defines the human need for connection above all else. Connection gives us life. As we sat, we were captivated by the information being presented—the deep water.

God created us to be in relationship, to be connected. First and foremost, we are to be connected to Him. That is pretty awesome—to be connected, in relationship, with the God of the universe. But it doesn't end there. We are designed, we need, to be connected to others. It is so essential that our entire nervous system's functioning depends on connecting with one another. Adam and Eve were two parts of the complete representation of God. The entirety of God demands that those two parts come together, to be in relationship, be in connection.

There is so much more to the theory, and I am certainly not doing it justice here, but I want to seed your mind with the possibilities of these thoughts. The functioning of our bodies is in direct correlation to our being in connection with others. Amazing. We are meant to be on the same team.

LOOSE LIPS SINK SHIPS

It's a latte in the Berlin mug and a quiet house and relevant deep water.

How do you define friendship? How do you know it exists? We've all known close friendships and friendships where you can go months or even years without contact and resume "right where you left off." But let's dig deeper …

Do your friendships honor that very title? Do those you call friends love at all times? Who are those friends that have celebrated with you and answered the call in adversity?

Too often, we use loose language. We call everyone we know our "friend," and we "love" our morning coffee. But I challenge you that those are not the deep, honest definitions behind our words. Friends, in the truest sense, celebrate with you and help bear your burdens. If a friend cannot do both, then perhaps it's time to redefine or rename the relationship.

> *"A friend loves at all times, and a brother is born for a time of adversity."*
>
> **Proverbs 17:17, ESV**

LET'S START AT THE VERY BEGINNING

Latte in hand. Wrapped in the pink summer robe. The sunrise is hidden behind light wispy clouds that reveal moments of subtle pinks and oranges and blues.

Yesterday's deep water lesson was a lengthy battle, hard-won. Almost two years of watching someone dear to me seek, turn the pages of their own life's book back and forth and back again. Ultimately, they ended up right where they'd begun and knew, in the deepest personal truth, that they were exactly where they needed to be all along. Walking alongside that struggle—guiding, cajoling, sometimes shouting the truth vehemently, was an exercise in my own personal patience and frustration, and I, for one, am elated to watch the result of this dear one's epiphany.

    I think about how God has had a few of these experiences Himself. The paternal wisdom, knowing the truth, laying out the perfect plan, only to have His children circle back in doubt and frustration. His example encourages those of us in guiding roles. Even when—especially when—those following balk at the wisdom and truth being shared. While yesterday's deep water lesson initially appeared to be for the person so dear to me, this morning's light reveals an even greater lesson for me ...

    If the God of Abraham, Isaac, and Jacob can stand in truth, strength, and patience while followers wander in their own wilderness, then I, too, should expect no less from Him concerning me. In that truth, there is ultimate joy.

THROWING FUEL ON THE FIRE

It's a plain ol' latte in the Graeter's mug and thunderstorms scaring the dogs and character building.

Have you ever been in a fight? What about an argument? In the middle of that disagreement, in the heat of the moment, have you ever acted "less than?" Have you chosen words that hurt or even been physically aggressive with the other person?

Here's something to consider: When we behave in a "less than" manner that causes harm to another, we are actually harming ourselves. We reduce our character to a base level. By not requiring more of ourselves in stressful moments, by acting out verbally or physically against someone else, damage is done to everyone involved.

It doesn't matter what another person is doing or saying in a disagreement; when you act out in a "less than" manner, it is at the expense of your character. And God has made you a better person than that.

WHERE? WHEN? WHY? HOW?

It's coffee with cream in the white mug and blankets and a hoodie and chilly morning deep water.

It's all about the timing. Yes. Sure. But perhaps there's more?

Presentation, taking your audience into account, has just as much impact as timing.

Telling any of the men in my life, "We need to talk," will most certainly cause concern, fear, stress, … you get the picture. Saying, "I'd like to talk about such-and-such, when can we make time today, tomorrow, or this week," opens a door. The door to communication and relationship. It allows them to lower their guard because they have a clue about what to expect.

Jesus didn't keep His topic of conversation a secret. He invited others into trustworthy communication. Even when His message was difficult or corrective, there was never a "gotcha" or "set-up." Healthy relationships do not avoid the hard stuff. Love speaks the truth. Wisdom, however, requires each of us to consider both when we present our requests and how.

CHOOSE LIFE

It's coffee with heavy cream in the NASA mug and dogs huddled up close and life-filled deep water.

The bestie pointed something out yesterday that floods my morning today. "Who is speaking life to you?" When we join with others and submit ourselves to the Christ in them, we have the great blessing of speaking and receiving life.

Don't get me wrong. I am not talking about rainbows and unicorns. I am speaking of calling out truth in love. This is about submitting ourselves to God's truth and Christ's love in and for one another. It is understanding that praising the good and condemning the sin are both kindness in action. It is all about making ourselves and one another into better people. Better Christ followers. Better representations of Christ himself.

Find your people. Stay accountable to them. Humble yourself to all they have to say about who God is and who you are in Him.

YOU'RE SO FUNNY

It's a keto coffee in the Miami Mom mug and two-sleeps-until-they're-home-excitement and protective deep water.

I don't tease. I just don't, even though I like a good joke as much as the next person. His ability to make me laugh is one of the reasons I love my Mac. Jokes, yes. Teasing, no.

I've often been called "too sensitive" for my position on teasing. After all, it's "just joking." But it's not. Getting a laugh at someone else's expense isn't what we are called to do or who we are called to be. It is not life.

> *"Like a madman who throws firebrands, arrows, and death is the man who deceives his neighbor and says, 'I am only joking!'"*
> **Proverbs 26:18-19, ESV**

> *"Let no corrupting talk come out of your mouths, but only such as is good for building up, as fits the occasion, that it may give grace to those who hear."*
> **Ephesians 4:29, ESV**

Speak life.

WALK WITH ME

It's a two-cup kind of day with rain and potentially game #2 of 6 for the week and heartfelt painful deep water.

Relationship—true, open relationship requires vulnerability. It asks both parties to have the sincerity and faith to speak truth and share difficulties. To celebrate joyful victories and kneel over hurts. True relationship asks us to be open to self-assessment and the possibility of required change.

It is a mature thing to enter into relationship.

When we offer ourselves (as individuals, as partners, as parents), we are requiring more. We are saying to the other, "I am willing to walk with you and hear you and share the truth in love." It is a promise to stay. To be involved even when the sharing is difficult. Even when the sharing forces us to see things we, perhaps, can't or don't want to see.

A relationship is a promise. I'm wondering today if our need for relationship is more for the times when things are difficult than when they are easy. I'm wondering if opening up to the "it takes a village" nature of relationships means falling more on our knees than it does the raising of our glasses.

WINNING AT ANY COST

It's an almond milk latte in the pink floral mug and humidity as thick as pea soup and a Catahoula on a cardboard hunt.

"Come dive deep with Me ..." He beckons.

I read a quote from that famous person named Unknown: "When any person thinks they are right and won't listen, they become out of control."

Do you know any great debaters? What is their motive? To win the argument. To be in control. And superficially, they may win. But here's the rub: in winning the argument, in "gaining control," they actually become out of control. The win sacrifices the one thing, the ultimate thing, for which we were made—relationship.

When you insist on being right, on winning the argument, you become a slave to that effort. You drive home your point by driving the person away as your heart is hardened to others. Ultimately, you are out of control because of your need to control. (Quite the oxymoron for so early in the day!)

Jesus gave us the perfect example of relationship. He sought the Father's will, in love, with every breath He took. He entered into relationship not to win an argument and prove He was correct (even though He was always correct), but to speak the truth in love and encourage others to do the same. He increased the Father's design, "It is not good for man to be alone." We were made, like the Trinity itself, to be in relationship.

Jesus was always in perfect relationship, but never fought for control—never sought to win. He knew the only one with that kind of control was the Father himself. Jesus was never out of control because of His heart for the Father and for His fellow man.

Control is never about love. It is the antithesis of love. Even in small things, the need to be right sacrifices the opportunity for all involved to learn and grow and become more. Speak the truth. In love. Not as an argument to win, but with the goal of growing—as individuals and in relationship.

BY ANY OTHER NAME

It's a K-cup coffee in the zebra mug and the last morning to sit with the water and the birdsong and "by any other name" deep water.

Looking for differences separates us. Finding similarities draws us together.

This week, the little and I have lived with family, but time and distance have made us all but strangers. There is a LOT of love and a lot of potential for differences.

My aunt and I were making dinner last night. As we chopped and sautéed, making her daughter's requested meal, the deep water snuck in.

We make the same recipe. We just call it by another name. I am different from her. She is different from me. And yet ...

Look for the similarities.

BE OUR GUEST

It's a second cardamom sugar latte in the pretty Poland mug and a fire to ward off the morning chill and finding a new rhythm.

We entertain. Often. Our goal for many years has been to have space in our home that will accommodate entertaining. One person. Lots of people. Put on the music. Pour the wine.

This morning's quiet time reading offered up a deep water shift from one of my many volumes of books: "The focus of entertaining is often the host rather than the guest ... True hospitality is all about the guest and their needs." So, maybe our heart has been one of hospitality and not entertaining. Semantics? Sure. But it got me thinking ...

How much hospitality do we extend to one another? In our homes? In our families? Isn't the goal to exemplify Christ, especially to our family members? In the training up. In the covenant with our spouse. Isn't it all about showing the love of Christ with all we have and in everything we do? Today, I am reminding myself "that hospitality is for the sake of honoring another." Today, this is my meditation:

> *"Be hospitable to one another without complaint."*
> 1 Peter 4:9, NASB

May we honor Christ in and for one another.

WHO YA' GONNA CALL?

It's the healthy mocha in a very well-worn Miami mom mug and the pretty pink robe and a day of decorating.

Have you ever been ghosted—abruptly cut off without communication or explanation? It's a perplexing experience. Being ghosted can open the door that leads to self-doubt. Or worse.

This morning's deep water is courtesy of Simon Senik. I paraphrase, "Ghosting is done by people who lack the skill for healthy confrontation."

Whether it is you doing the ghosting or you being ghosted, it's eye-opening to realize that this experience, which now has its own Urban Dictionary name, is all about an inability to speak the truth in love. To say the hard things with a gentle voice and an open heart.

When I wrote this, we were preparing for the Christmas season, which is so easily filled with family discord, unmet expectations, and stress. God reminded me to keep in mind that speaking the truth in love is an act of maturity. Something He has modeled for us, graced us for, and equipped us to do. Let's reach for that instead of cold silence or passive-aggressive comments in the face of conflict.

I COULDN'T CARE LESS

It's an airport latte in a paper cup and already missing Mimi duty and Hallmark moments of truth.

It's from the film Ghosts of Girlfriends Past, where Connor Mead says, "I learned that the ultimate power in a relationship lies with the one who cares less."

Hmmm ... the one who cares less ...

If you can take it or leave it, perhaps you do hold the power. But what a sad position in which to find one's self: to NOT care just enough. What a precipice.

What if Jesus were the one who didn't care enough?

I am not totally sure what today's deep water is trying to teach me, but at the very least, please don't let me be the one who doesn't care enough.

CH–CH–CH–CHANGES

It's an on-plan strawberry lemonade in Grammie's green glass and Sunday sports and party clean up.

God's been changing up my people. Holding tight to the few. Adding some new. This morning's deep water had lots to say about it.

The company you keep 100% impacts who you are and what you do. We do not live in a vacuum. These new people I'm blessed to call friends aren't there by accident. They make me a better me.

Take stock. Do the people you live with, the videos you watch, the music and podcasts you listen to point you in the direction of health? Do they lift you up? Are they speaking life? If not, maybe it's time to make a change.

GIVE ME MORE

It's a second oatmeal latte in a second cup because the first ended up all over the fluffy pink winter robe and the weekend! ... and a heart's yearning for deeper.

After a lifetime of travel and moving more times than I can count, I'm jealous for the opportunity to grow and deepen relationships with my aunts. I am learning the depth of who they are and their hearts, and I want more.

Today's deep water is another layer from one of these beloved women. She and I share more than I ever realized. She and I are more alike than perhaps either of us anticipated. She is generous beyond measure, and I am grateful for her.

"Share joy. Double joy.

Share sorrow. Half sorrow.

Remember me whether you're happy or worried."

She shared this Swedish proverb with me. She was vulnerable in it. She is so beautiful. I am blessed beyond measure to remember her always, happy or worried.

Remember. Happy or worried.

DIFFERENT STROKES FOR DIFFERENT FOLKS

It's a glass of red in one of my great grandmother's goblets and post-surgery peaceful rest and missing my Mac.

Some days, I am amazed.

Today, I got to sit with a member of my A-team. One of the founding members. We sat. And we talked. Real talk. Questions and answers. Seeking to understand. And I am … I was amazed.

You see, we are different in so many ways. Our life maps are as different as oil and water. But we love one another, so that always trumps the differences. And today, I learned. I learned that my "different" is also her "different." That in those very different experiences exists good and well and love and fulfillment.

I once saw our differences as gaps, rivers, and caverns between us that separated us and marked a divide. Instead, I now see they are just differences. Nothing to keep us apart. Nothing to separate. Just different.

What if differences aren't obstacles? What if they are opportunities? What if they are places to understand and connect? What if those rivers and caverns bring joy?

> *"There is a river whose streams make glad the city of God…"*
>
> **Psalm 46:4a, ESV**

YOU'RE STUCK WITH ME

It's an afternoon latte in the pretty Poland mug to warm up and a new-ish game partner and adventure time.

There's an African proverb that says: "If you want to go fast, go alone. If you want to go far, go together."

I am seeing the things and taking it all in with one of the A-team today. We've been in this for the long haul. We're definitely better together.

Find your long-haul warriors. Like Naomi and Ruth. "Where you go, I will go. And your people will be my people." Living life together is one of the many blessings of living a life of faith. They make you better. Stronger.

> "Two are better than one, because they have a good reward for their toil. For if they fall, one will lift up his fellow. But woe to him who is alone when he falls and has not another to lift him up! Again, if two lie together, they keep warm, but how can one keep warm alone? And though a man might prevail against one who is alone, will withstand him—a threefold cord is not quickly broken."
>
> **Ecclesiastes 4:9-12, ESV**

MARRIAGE

Marriage is the very first mission field. A space where the deep water reveals our beauty and our brokenness. A space where the best in me loves the worst in you and vice versa. This is the place where the promise of love lays the groundwork for personal growth and sanctification. The selfless love of marriage is the ideal place to demonstrate God's perfect love. Where else are we so vulnerable? Where else does someone see the worst in us and love us still? It is divine mercy in action. This is not the action of doing all the right things. This is the action of being the spouse God has called you to be and holding fast to the promises of today, tomorrow, and forever.

ARRANGED MARRIAGE

It's a glass of spilled black currant iced tea and Rolfing—whatever the heck that is—and Catholic channel deep water.

"Every marriage is an arranged marriage."

What? I had to let that sink in. What in the world? But it's true. Even when, especially when, we are choosing our spouse. I am not talking about two sets of parents arranging a marriage between their children. I am speaking of the agreement between the youthful me and my youthful partner, arranging a marriage for our future, older selves. The people we will become. We are arranging the marriage of those two, who are not the people at the altar.

Mind. Blown.

HOSTAGE NEGOTIATIONS

The house is quiet. The sleepover people are still asleep. The coffee is waiting lest the coffee maker wake anyone.

This morning's deep water is about love and hostages. We fall in love with people for who they are and how they make us feel. A mature love grown over time recognizes what "things" make our spouse feel most loved (i.e., their Love Language), and we love in that "language" more and more. However.

However. Demanding our spouse act (therefore love us) in a certain way is not the selfless love of the Bible. It is selfish. At best, it is selfish. When we say, "If you loved me. you would_____," we hold the other person hostage. Love doesn't demand how it is expressed. Love can demand right, good, and moral living, but it doesn't demand a particular expression.

That said ... there's always more, isn't there? While it isn't fair, reasonable, or healthy to demand a spouse love in a certain way to prove their love, it's equally unhealthy to ignore what the other truly needs and what makes them feel most loved. It's a fine line, but it does exist. For example, I know my husband likes sweet tea to drink. Because I love him, I try to keep sweet tea made. I try. And he appreciates it when he can open the refrigerator and grab that tea. Here's the fine line—I offer the tea. When or if he demands that I make sweet tea to prove my love to him, it would cross the line. That would be manipulation. That would be holding love hostage, and that has nothing to do with whether or not I love him.

> *"Love cares more for others than for self ... Love doesn't want what it doesn't have ... Doesn't keep score ..."*
>
> 1 Corinthians 13:4-5, MSG

AN ACCOUNTING ERROR

No cup of anything today—just diving straight into the deep water.

What are you doing to build up your house? What are you doing to tear it down? I'm going to venture a guess that pride is integral in the answer.

Marriage is a gift requiring more work than many of us ever imagined. The promises of youth often morph into challenges more difficult than we bargained for and blessings richer than we ever dreamt. In the midst of all the living we're doing, it's worth it to take inventory of what we're contributing to our most important earthly relationship.

Are you giving up personal pride to build up your spouse? Is "being right" or "doing it a better way" contributing to your marital harmony or damaging the relationship? Sometimes, we need to realize that even if we are able, deferring to our spouse's wishes or even honoring a request in spite of our ability to do it may be a step the other needs. Just because you can doesn't always mean you should. We all know the "I can load the dishwasher better" scenario ... Pause for a moment and consider how many times you imply or directly show you can do something better at the expense of the other. Unless it's biblical, moral, or financial, I'm going to offer that preserving your spouse's heart and sense of ability is far more important than doing "it"—whatever your "it" is—the best.

TAKE UP YOUR MANTLE

It's an Arnold Palmer in a Chick-fil-A® cup and salt and water (a.k.a. sweat) and dogs playing hard in the cooler weather.

The deep water came to us during our study time today. Break out the Bible and be amazed at how fast and hard God shows up!

Men are the leaders, the providers, the protectors. Adam was a leader, provider, protector. Or was he? Was he leading Eve in the Garden? Was he providing for her in the Garden? Was he protecting her from the taunts and haunts of Satan?

Maybe we got it wrong? Maybe?

Ladies, I'm not trying to usurp our spouse's role as leader, provider, protector. I advocate as strongly as I can for a benevolent patriarchal leadership model in the home. There are two spouses with equal responsibility and equal ability, but God's Word is clear that the husband is responsible to God for himself, his wife, and his children. That said, maybe our spouse isn't "the" leader, provider, and protector to whom we should have been/should be looking.

When we make the altar of matrimony our source of strength and protection, we make marriage an idol. When we look to our spouse to lead us, provide for us, and protect us, is it possible that we are imposing our need for God onto our spouse? And what if our husband isn't up for the ultimate role of leader, provider, and protector? To whom shall we go as women, as wives, as mothers?

If you find yourself, as many women do, in a place absent a clear leading in God's will, seek God. Perhaps this is a season where, like many of the women in Acts, you are called to lead. Like Mary, the mother of Jesus, you are called to act alongside others in the formation of a church.[1] Or maybe you are called to be like Tabitha, caring for the widows and

---

1. See Acts 1:12-26.

the poor.² Or are you to be like Mary, the mother of John Mark, and Rhoda, her jubilant servant girl, and joyfully open your home as a place of fellowship and ministry?³ And maybe, just maybe, you are called to emulate the wealthy and powerful Lydia of Thyatira, the first Christian convert in what is now Europe, and use your provision and status to influence businessmen and politicians in the spread of the Gospel.⁴

If you find yourself without clear provision, seek God. Are you being asked or required to step out and fill the role of family provider (for a season or a lifetime)? If you find yourself without spiritual protection, seek God. His Word tells us we have direct access to the powers to defeat Satan and his army. Direct access. Warriors. You see, our heavenly Father is the perfect example of all these attributes. Our spouses are not excused from their roles, but they aren't the heavenly embodiment of them either. Rather than settle for lack, take time to sit with the perfect Bridegroom and let Him share His love and provision and plan for your life.

> *"... there is no male and female, for you are all one in Christ Jesus."*
>
> **Galatians 3:28b, ESV**

---

2. See Acts 9:36-43.
3. See Acts 12:6-19.
4. See Acts 16:11-40.

STAY IN THE GAME

It's iced mint tea and rain and deep water. Water so deep you need waders ...

> *"In the middle of an emotional upset, when you walk away, you do two things—you abandon your partner, and you assume control." (The Gottman Institute).*

Ouch. What happened to the cooperation and partnership of marriage? If you aren't staying in the game, if you aren't working toward a solution in the midst of tough times, you are actually abandoning your partner. Or, worse yet, you are taking control. Not in a healthy way, but literally taking control from your partner, rendering them weak. Placing them in a subservient position.

God's design for marriage is to complement one another. To work—in love—to bring out the best in each other. When we don't engage in the relationship—in relating to one another, even when relating is monumentally challenging—we are working to upset God's design. This is one of the many reasons God's Word commands us to resolve moments of difference and righteous anger in a timely fashion. Relating is building up, not abandoning or controlling. Fight the good fight.

> *"In your anger do not sin:" Do not let the sun go down while you are still angry ...*
>
> **Ephesians 4:26, NIV**

FARMERS UNITE

It's a Starbucks® morning and rain and cooler weather and deep water sneaking in as moments of truth.

The Mac and I leave for a weeklong marriage retreat tomorrow. In the middle of running errands and pre-trip preparation, my Central Market cashier handed me some pretty serious deep water.

"Any special plans for the weekend?" he asked.

"Actually, yes. My husband and I are going on a marriage retreat."

"Good for you. We need people working on their marriage. Especially in this day and age, you know what I mean?"

"Yes. Yes, I do," I replied.

"People often say the grass is always greener. I've also heard the grass is only green where seeds are planted ..."

Hmmmm. Do the work. Plant the seeds.

> *"Wives, submit to your own husbands, as to the Lord ... Husbands, love your wives, as Christ loved the church and gave Himself up for her ... This mystery is profound ..."*
>
> **Ephesians 5:22-33, ESV**

FIRST COMES LOVE, THEN COMES MARRIAGE

It's the (whatever beverage) in the (whatever cup) and the deep water lessons on the Greatest Commandment.

> *Jesus said unto him, "Thou shalt love the Lord thy God with all thy heart, and with all thy soul, and with all thy mind." This is the first and great commandment. And the second is like unto it, "Thou shalt love thy neighbor as thyself." On these two commandments hang all the law and the prophets."*
>
> **Matthew 22:37-39, KJV**

First, love God. Second, love others.

No more. No less.

I recently asked one of our priests what one should do when loving someone seems to contradict speaking the truth in love.

First, love God. Second, love others.

"Will 'speaking the truth in love' have a positive (for their betterment) effect?" he asked.

"No. I don't believe it will," I answered.

"Well then, first love God. Then, love others. When we love others, we do not cause them harm. If speaking the truth in love will not have a positive (for their betterment) outcome, then we wait until there is an appropriate time to speak the truth. Until then, we love."

Sometimes, what is left unsaid is the most appropriate expression of genuine love.

LANGUAGE BARRIERS

It's a cardamom latte in a paper cup and the summer robe because ... summer ... and deep water with the A-team.

Do you know your love language? Primary? Secondary? Do you know your spouse's love language(s)? Have we opened the door and solved at least this relational puzzle? Do we all now know how we need to be loved to feel loved? Yay us!

Or not.

I'm sure the authors of The 5 Love Languages books were completely altruistic. I'm sure their goal was to establish healthy self-awareness and equip people in relationships how to love each other well. I'm also equally sure we are now held hostage to loving one another "as we need to be loved."

When did knowing what you need completely trump the wonderful ways your spouse demonstrates love to you and for you if/when that loving isn't done "in your love language"? When did knowing your spouse's love language devalue the inherent way you love others and the way they love you?

I'm on a bit of a tangent here. But it's huge. Yes, loving another should mean a willingness to understand and meet their needs. It's being other-focused. It's being invested and aware and selfless. But that isn't the end game. It just isn't. And if I devalue all the wonderful ways my husband loves me simply because it isn't done "in my love language," I'm sure to miss all the wonderful ways I am loved. All the wonderful ways he expresses his love to me in ways that are unique to him.

Fill one another's cups. To overflowing. Both for the other person and out of who you are, the way God created you. If He put the two of you together, I'm sure there's a reason you love the way you do and it is good.

> "... give preference to one another in honor ..."
> **Romans 12:10b, NASB**

BIGGER. BETTER. FASTER. STRONGER.

It's a soon-to-be-enjoyed glass of Pino in a proper glass and having the A/C on in October and thematic deep water.

God has been pressing me to consider gratitude. And a spirit of poverty. And this plague-like modernist trend of wanting more, wanting better … wanting, wanting, wanting.

I've seen (via FaceBook) three marriages dissolve this year. The ever-glossy FaceBook world left me shocked when the marriages dissolved and new marriages were celebrated. I continue to be challenged by this nagging neediness.

How often do we look for or leave behind something good (not just in marriage or relationships), hoping for something better? How often do we realize, taillights in the mirror, that what wasn't good enough was actually the "better" we were hoping for all along?

I don't know any specifics concerning your situation. I don't know what "better" you may be hoping to find. What I do know is that shiny things tarnish, precious glass gets chipped, and the grass is pretty darned green if you water it right where you are.

Before you are too quick to bail on what you have, consider if you have nurtured it well and given it a chance to flourish as God intended.

THE WORST OF TIMES

It's a cardamom latte in the Seghesio mug and the pretty pink winter robe and cleaning day.

Rom-Com spoiler alert: there is no happily-ever-after ending.

The deep water defines love in such a solid way this morning. Love is not about the fuzzy feeling you get in your tummy and your toes. Love is not about the fantastic date nights, or a romantic home-cooked meal eaten by candlelight, or the most thoughtful gift ever. Love is not all the wonderful moments that Hollywood and Disney want us to believe.

Love is not a feeling. It is not an emotion.

Love. Love is a choice. A choice we make in the in-between times. Love is the choice we make when none of the romance, none of the pretty, is present.

> *"(Love is) being there when someone's damage makes them seem impossible. Knowing that they are so much more than their worst moments."*
>
> **Dr. Dre**

A HAPPY HOUSE

It's a plain ol' latte in the William & Mary mug and sleepless nights and drinking in the wisdom.

My aunt is my firehose of life and love these days. I am looking for those moments when I can glean something new, something life-giving, something to make me smile.

During our recent girls' weekend, my aunt shared something that will forever change how we do things in our house. A paradigm shift is in play.

"Instead of happy wife, happy life, how about happy spouse, happy house?"

I'm sure the good book might agree …

> *"Be subject to one another out of reverence for Christ."*
>
> **Ephesians 5:21, NCB**

HOME IMPROVEMENTS

It's a keto-friendly coffee in the "there's a chance this is wine" mug and Midwest humidity and the pretty pink summer robe to start the day.

I remind him how handsome he is. I still tell him how crazy beautiful his blue eyes are. I thank him for all he has done and continues to do to provide us with a wonderful quality of life. I giggle with him like a schoolgirl. I bat my eyes at him.

He takes me out to dinner. He makes my coffee … often. He takes me on trips he knows I will enjoy. He does a million little things, including watering my flowers in the heat of summer so I can enjoy their beauty. He buys me flowers and cooks me dinner.

Through all the really tough times, we continue to date one another and flirt with one another. They are, in my mind, the most significant things we have done to preserve our marriage.

We truly are better together.

BALANCING THE BUDGET

It's a Lot 38 Café Viennese in a paper cup and getting answers to the questions and looking forward to the end of another day of flying.

If you're married or you are in a relationship, how are your finances?

The deep water offered up one of the best pieces of financial advice I've encountered in a long time.

Never forget that marriage is like a bank account. You always want to deposit more than you take out. And if you overdraw your deposits, there will be fees to pay.

Hmmm.

Here's to depositing.

I LOST THE GAME

It's a healthy mocha in the Ikea blue glass and sleeping wherever the paint is not and making up for all the humidity we didn't have in Alaska.

There is one right. There is one wrong. And therein lies all the stress of being a right-fighter. You either win. Or you lose.

That might make for a great debate or a win in a courtroom, but it certainly doesn't make for a good relationship. It doesn't make for healthy internal dialogue, either. Oh, the personal shame and condemnation from believing you must either be right or you will be wrong.

The deep water is unraveling a lifetime of wrong thinking. It's kind of like detangling a slinky that's in knots. Wrong thinking can and will entrench itself in, around, and back on itself until you'd be hard-pressed to set it straight again. More than one thing can be true at the same time. As it turns out, grey is a beautiful color, and black-and-white thinking carries an air of legalism that is toxic to the soul.

There are hard truths. I'm not talking about those. I'm pulling on the strings of making loving myself and loving others the most important task. Not being right. Not making another wrong. Fighting the good fight is what Jesus was all about. The good fight is fighting for love. Love isn't right or wrong. Love simply is.

> *"Be devoted to one another in love ..."*
> Romans 12:10a, NASB

THE MOUTHS OF BABES

It's a peppermint water in a plastic bottle and sunny Sunday porch sitting and looking for the new house.

I was tuned out in Mass today. Foggy. Distracted. "I didn't really get anything out of the readings today," I shared. "Maybe just the stuff about being called into a life of service. That marriage is a life of service. A life of service to your spouse."

The not-so-little middle threw a pivotal curveball my way. "It's actually a life of service to the marriage, not the person."

Deep water mic drop.

> *"... give preference to one another in honor."*
> **Romans 12:10b, NASB**

PARENTING

Parenting is a journey through deep waters—sometimes calm and peaceful, the safety of the shore in sight. At other times, stormy seas, uncharted territory, and overwhelming responsibility. Even with all of the sacrifice, challenges, and difficult (impossible) moments, there is nothing on this planet that can quite compare to the joy this brings. We are given the great privilege of walking beside our children—teaching, loving, and preparing them. Ultimately, though, their journey is theirs to chart. In these parenting moments filled with uncertainty, growth, and faith, we find our greatest lessons—not just for our children, but for ourselves. Through joys, struggles, and inevitable goodbyes, parenting calls us to live with love, intention, and trust in the bigger picture. Our greatest role is not to control the outcome but to faithfully live out the example we hope they will follow.

FOR EXAMPLE

It's a blue Solo® cup filled with room temperature water and the smell of bleach and a few moments of quiet while the Mac and the boys are at the waterpark.

Father's Day had me thinking, What makes a good father? That snowballed into, What makes a good parent?

And like a flood, there came the deep water. As a Christian, my first thought was that teaching your children about God and Jesus and faith would be the priority. Then, a whole bunch of very practical notions about living in the world and being a productive member of society came to mind. I had lots and lots of thoughts and questions about the hows and whys of parenting.

Then God laid the deep water trump card in front of me. The most important job in parenting is how we live. The example that we set. What better way to teach our children about God, about Jesus, about their faith, about relationships with others, about how to handle stress, about how to deal with anger and disappointment, about how to steward money than the example of how we live? Maybe if we stop trying so hard to tell our children how to live and be and do and instead live our own lives as Christ followers, our example would compel our children to do likewise.

> *"Dedicate your children to God and point them in the way that they should go, and the values they've learned from you will be with them for life."*
>
> **Proverbs 22:6, TPT**

HOWLING AT THE MOON

It's a second glass of cabernet and football and awesome deep water.

"Sorry I'm back so soon," announced the little after an abbreviated walk with Doug-the-dog, "there was a coyote."

The Mac and I laughed. Literally. While we do have coyotes in Texas, neither of us could really believe the boy had encountered one in our neighborhood. And in the midst of laughs and joking and teasing, the deep water.

"Come on," the Mac summoned. "Let's go see this coyote."

There was the moment when the little's father—the Mac—recognized a need to set the situation right. He and his son went together to investigate the threat. And if there really is a coyote, you better bet the Mac will protect his son. The little is in good hands. If no coyote is to be found, the little will walk through the assurance of learning that even when the threat is only perceived, his daddy will be there.

Our heavenly Father is the same. We come to Him with perceived threats—anxieties over things that will most likely never befall us—and even in the midst of unlikely possibilities, He reaches for us, investigates, and assures us all is well. All will be well.

EVERYTHING IS AWESOME

It's another almond milk latte in the Oh Happy Day mug and finally-asleep sleepover quiet and end of an era deep water.

We are officially over LEGO® sets. After 20 years of having at least one, if not many, LEGO® boxes under our Christmas tree, this year, we have none. It makes my heart heavy. The excitement of "What is it this year?" isn't this year. The anticipation of brothers sitting together, working together, and learning together for at least a few hours every Christmas afternoon will not be this year. A tradition is ending, and until this morning, I'm not sure I was aware it was an actual tradition.

I might be a bit of a rebel and find some LEGO® boxes for them, just to keep the tradition alive. More often than not, we give the things people want/like/need. This year, I'm going to give what I need—to see these boys-becoming-men stay connected. To experience the joy of their combined efforts and the product of having boys in my home.

I want to walk into a bedroom and see yet another LEGO® Star Wars ship on a shelf and, for a moment, hold them all right here with me, in this home, little boys who want nothing more than to play with LEGO® bricks.

> *"To everything there is a season, and a time for every purpose under heaven."*
>
> **Ecclesiastes 3:1, KJV**

Let the season of LEGO® magic continue!

WHO KNEW?

The sweet tea with a splash of lemonade got left on the counter and the carpool line is incredibly long considering it is still 45 minutes before dismissal. Sometimes you learn lessons that are more than you ever anticipated and you are grateful.

Of course, I knew my heart would love my children. What I didn't know until 22 years into the process was that it would be my most important job. There were so many "Should-do" tasks, loving my boys and loving them well feels like it often got put on the back burner.

Each Sunday when we go to Mass, we hear about the first and greatest commandment and the second like unto it, and it is shockingly new to me that loving my children is significantly more important than making them into some predetermined outcome. Loving them for who they are and how God created them and loving them through the ups and downs and differences of life. Loving them, not to a superimposed standard, but just simply loving them.

> "Your most important job as a parent is to love your child. Love them hard. Love them deeply. Love them always."
>
> Christine Crockett Smith

FOREVER TOGETHER, YOU AND ME

The wine has been drunk and the dark has overtaken the day and the deep water seeps in between the cracks.

Be still and know ...

Life will overwhelm you. It will demand and command your every second of every minute of every hour of every day. Another one of Satan's great tricks is to keep 'em running, and they won't have anything left to see God. If he can't make you stray, he'll make you busy.

The little has been my centering point lately. Two weeks at camp and a cross-country move and he is growing into seeking time with his mom. Moments. Conversations. Sharing life. He reminds me to sit and be still. "Can we just be? Together?"

Yes, son. Just being. Together. What a beautiful, wonderful, amazing thing you are offering me.

> *Jesus said, "Let the little children come to Me, and do not hinder them, for the kingdom of heaven belongs to such as these."*
> **Matthew 19:14, NIV**

TEACH YOUR CHILDREN WELL

It's a cool San Pellegrino on a hot day and host prep and love-based deep water.

Today is infusion day. I have Multiple Sclerosis, and there is a lot going on this week, but everything stops for the medicine that keeps me going. This is the only mom the little has ever known—the one who needs infusions. It has influenced who he is and how he lives.

I was greeted by a loving welcome note and a latte and San Pellegrino and gherkins when I returned home from my infusion today. The little had done all his chores (and more), done them well, and made me quite the spread. He knows my love languages—words of affirmation and acts of service. He knows the exhausting impact Tysabri can have on me. In the absence of anyone else to care for me and love on me, he filled the void.

Humble amazement. Epic deep water.

If we teach our children to be good workers, they will work. If we teach our children to be good servants, they will serve. If we demonstrate Christ to our children, they will love.

> *"Let all that you do be done in love."*
> **1 Corinthians 16:14, ESV**

THE EQUIPMENT CLOSET

The sun is up. The morning is miserably hot and humid even for Texas. It's espresso with almond milk vanilla creamer. And the bus is long gone.

Today's deep water involved walking two of the three dogs. As parents, we are so busy trying to make sure our children have everything they need to ensure their success that we often overlook our role, our personal role, in shaping who they'll become.

It is not our role to make sure we have godly children. It is our role to make sure our children have godly parents. You can equip your children with everything they "need" to be successful, but if you aren't seeking every day to be the best God wants you to be, you may be missing the biggest parenting mark out there.

> *"And above all these put on love, which binds everything together in perfect harmony."*
>
> **Colossians 3:14, ESV**

ADLERIAN PSYCHOLOGY 101

It's a packet of lime Pruvit with San Pelligrino and counting everything and light layers for a sunny day's hike.

We had it out yesterday. Shared our frustrations, our hurts, our wants, and our caring. Tears. Lines crossed. Bridges built. Relationship is work.

The deep water is work. Good work, but work nonetheless.

It is my sincere belief that parents should do the absolute best for their children with everything they have. A lot or a little, visible or invisible, parents love their kiddos. I also believe (or have at least uttered often enough to be a "thing") that even in doing my very best, I will somehow hurt my children. It may be a harsh word or not listening or not understanding when they so desperately needed me to. It may be putting my baggage on them. It may be missing the subtle cues. It will not be harm by intent, but we are human, and we act in ways that can and do negatively impact others. Children are no exception.

Why, I wonder, do we so often try to force our children into our preconceived molds? Why do we insist we know best when, maybe, just maybe, we don't? Why are we more apt to try and change the floundering child instead of considering what they truly need is to have their environment changed?

Maybe I need to consider my defined goals for my boys. Maybe I need to reconsider how I parent. Maybe I need to be the grownup and recognize when "how we do things in this house" may not be, is often not, the best for a child.

The work of yesterday has taught me that being open to how another sees things, what another needs, and putting aside my own perspective for their highest and best is the most loving way forward. I won't disregard the truth, but I will consider there may be another, an additional, way of getting there. Parenting is a high calling.

> *"... walk in a manner worthy of the calling to which you have been called, with all humility and gentleness, with patience, bearing one another in love."*
>
> **Ephesians 4:1b-2, ESV**

MAKIN' A SCENE

It's a citrus LMNT water in the pink tumbler and rainy days and Mondays and cosy clothes and big fluffy slippers for doing all the things and stuff.

Toddlers are really great communicators. Truly. Ever seen a toddler drop to the ground, arms and legs flailing, doing their best to tell you they have not been heard sufficiently? Who better to light you up and let you know they do not feel seen than a toddler?

We all know giving in to the wants and wishes of a toddler, however loudly and thoroughly communicated, is not always the best course of action. Quite the contrary. Just because we want something doesn't always (or often) mean it's good for us. Enter the deep water …

When we don't feel seen, we will often make a scene.

Read that one again.

Toddlers. Teens. Adults. This one does not discriminate based on age. One need only turn on the news, look at social media, or, heck, go out in public to see someone making sure with a grand display that everyone knows they do not feel seen.

The inherent disconnect of social media only serves to make the lack of being seen more intense. More acute. Despite being "connected" 24/7, we are less connected than ever. The relationship we deeply desire (I'd say require) moves farther and farther away from us, leaving many to flail about very publicly.

"See me! See me!"

The void we are experiencing in this less-than-connected world looks a lot like a toddler in full-on tantrum mode. We want what we want, and we want everyone to want it for us and with us and, as my father would say, "Katie, bar the door" on anyone who would dare say no.

It doesn't matter if the "no" is for our ultimate good or not. When we don't feel seen, we become desperate. When we don't feel seen, we make a scene.

One of the best ways I've learned to help settle a temper tantrum is to listen. To be calm in the midst of the storm. To get eye-to-eye and heart-to-heart and ask questions about what is wanted or needed. Not to say yes necessarily, but to have the conversation. Sometimes, getting a "yes" isn't necessary; just being heard and seen is enough.

GROWING UP

It's a cardamom latte in the Seghesio mug and beginning the day with stars and the pretty pink floral robe.

Spoiler alert: I don't do or see things in a typical fashion.

I have my moments, and I have a few trusted A-team members with whom I confess and share them, but for the most part, I see things differently than most of the world.

People. My boys are growing up. The boy has grown and flown. The not-so-little middle is just about to follow in his footsteps. And the little is about to jump into high school. You know what the majority of my heart says right now?

Yay!!!

Yes, I do have moments when my heart aches, but day in and day out, I'm grateful and excited. We have done what we are supposed to do—we've raised them to be men—outside our home, competently and confidently living their own lives in this world.

When the little goes off to college, I'm sure I'll shed a few tears. I'm sure I'll also stand beside the Mac, and we'll smile and start planning our next trip. To celebrate.

Instead of wishing our children would never grow up, what if we approached it with the attitude of "I'm so glad I get to see you grow up"? When they step into independence, it is a testament to a parenting job well done.

FLYING THE NEST

It's the pink Stanley full of LMNT citrus water and a box of tissues and indoor rainy days.

It is so wild, this pendulum between "Yay! We did it!" and "Oh my gosh, it's over ... It's really over."

The last day of high school. You are never really prepared for these moments, are you? No matter how much you plan and anticipate, suddenly, the big thing is upon you, and ... gulp, here we go! He doesn't officially graduate until next week. So, is it really here, this ending? Can I stall the truth of it by skirting the technicality of dates and diplomas?

Today, I'm crying a bit. Because I am so dang proud of this now young man. Because I actually like having him at home (most of the time). Because God has called him to big things, and I will miss seeing how those things unfold on the daily.

Today, I'm crying a bit. Because I prayed for this. From the moment he was born, I prayed for him to grow and learn and leap and fly. And here it is. The answer (at least in part) to those prayers.

Tears of joy mingle with tears of longing. Longing for the days of him being little and days of his adult-sized bear hugs. Joy for all that I have been able to share and see and witness and celebrate.

The deep water is a warm blanket today. It wraps around me to remind and encourage ... Don't be sad because it's over. Be glad because it happened.

The deep water gently, ever-so-softly speaks to me. It is for this that he was given to you.

> *"Be watchful, stand firm in the faith, act like men, be strong. Let all that you do be done in love."*
>
> 1 Corinthians 16:13-14, ESV

It is for this you have labored. It is for this you give him to God and the world and rejoice.

OPEN WIDE

It's the now routine mocha in the grateful mug and the song of so so many songbirds and new pretty pink pajamas hidden under the fluffy pink robe.

The not-so-little middle is getting married this year.

And suddenly, the deep water is not just about letting go—but opening wide.

Parenting teaches us, over and over, that love is not a closed circle. It's an ever-widening ripple. We pour ourselves into these little people—holding, guiding, correcting, praying, and sometimes just staying out of the way as they grow into who God made them to be. We imagine all the milestones. First steps. First games. First heartbreaks. First job. First apartment.

But I didn't imagine this moment.

The day he would say, "She's the one."

And I would know, deep in my gut, that he was right.

There's a girl—no, a woman—who has chosen him. Who knows his quirks and his heart and his loyalty and said yes. And he chose her, not just with words but with a lifetime promise already written on his face when he talks about her.

And just like that, our family gets bigger. Not just in size, but in love.

The deep water here feels different—more like a tributary of a river that carries us into a new body of water altogether. There is grief, yes. The kind that comes when something is beautiful and the change is bittersweet. The boy who once needed me to reach the top shelf now reaches for a bride's hand and says, "Come with me."

But there is also joy. So much joy.

We've prayed for this woman for years without even knowing her name. We've hoped for someone who would love him, challenge him, laugh with him, and run toward God beside him.

And now, we get to welcome her into the fold. A daughter.

This boy mom now gets to find out what it is like to mother a girl.

The not-so-little middle is getting married.

And the deep water rolls on—wider, richer, fuller than ever.

It is for this that he was raised.

And for this, we give thanks.

THE CHARACTER OF GOD

The character of God is marked by His relentless pursuit of us, deep compassion for us, and unwavering faithfulness to us. He is a good God who gives good things to His children. He does not delight in our suffering, but He does allow us to walk through fiery trials, promising that we will not be consumed and pass through the deep waters, promising that we will not drown. He knows that in them, we will come to know Him more fully. He seeks us in our brokenness, loves us through our defiance, and rejoices at our return.

"When you walk through the waters, I will be with you; and through the rivers, they shall not overwhelm you; when you walk through the fire, you shall not be burned, and the flame shall not consume you."

Isaiah 43:2, ESV

HOARDING

It's a cool morning and a 2- or 3-cuppa kind of morning.

The Catahoula has decided today is a day of mayhem. Four different shoes, the little's flashlight, a large stick, and paws full of black mulch. Each time he came to me I offered, "Where's your bone?"

I knew he had a better option than the mischief he was creating, and yet he persisted. "Where's your bone, Doug?" I was gentle. I encouraged. I demanded.

He wanted nothing to do with his bone.

Then, the deep water. Aren't we just like this not-so-adorable puppy? Don't we wander, finding our own way, demanding what we've found is the best option? I, for one, am thoroughly grateful God waits upon us patiently, knowing He is our best option. Even when—especially when—we bring Him all our other choices. He is THE choice.

THE ONE NOT HERE

It's an early afternoon cola with extra ice and spring planting and welcoming deep water.

As a military family, we are familiar with homecomings. We know the joy of greeting the one who has been gone and the exuberance of the one who has been waiting.

A recent photo op to share the new porch railing reminded me of waiting for the "one not here" to return. If you look closely at the glass front door, you can see Doug the dog, waiting for his people to return. He waits—without demands, without expectation. He waits with hope.

We are in the season of Lent, and as I watch Doug at his post, I am reminded of how much my Heavenly Father anticipates my return to Him, to faith, and to love.

> "So the Lord must wait for you to come to Him so He can show you His love and compassion. For the Lord is a faithful God..."
>
> **Isaiah 30:18a, NLT**

HEARTACHE AND HEARTBREAK

It's a healthy pumpkin spice latte in the New Orleans mug and jumping back into things and down deep in my guts deep water.

"Who told you that you were naked?"

How did that just sound to you? In your head?

How that question sounded—the voice, the tone, and the emphasis says a lot. So much more than I ever knew or understood before today.

Was that voice harsh? Critical? Condemning? Did you feel scolded?

Or was it empathetic? Saddened for you? Sorrowful? Did you feel seen?

That, dear ones, speaks one whole heck of a lot about how you see our Heavenly Father.

It was immediate. My answer. I heard the deepest, sternest, harshest voice. One of criticism and condemnation. How could you?!!!!!! But what if …

What if that voice was and is truly one of love? What if, rather than anger, that voice spoke with sorrow and heartbreak? The kind of voice you would respond with if you found your child hiding under the porch, ashamed because their friend told them that putting peroxide on their hair would turn it a beautiful shade of beach blonde instead of a horrible shade of brittle orange. "Aw, baby, who told you …?"

The deepest grief of a loving parent who understands the consequences of the choice and wants to undo it for you? Wants to take it all back or at least give a papa bear thumpin' to the one who led you down that path?

Imagine a love that deep.

Today, my eyes are open to a new version of the story. My eyes are open to the very real love of a parent who didn't criticize or condemn, but loved so very much they cursed the one who led a beloved child astray and made a way for them to come all the way back.

May we all know that kind of love.

A DOG'S LIFE

It's an Advent calendar espresso and foamed milk in the Miami mom mug and two fireplaces to warm our space and another day of organizing (because Covid)!

The deep water has gone to the dogs. Literally. Bella, in true St. Bernard fashion, took her sweet ol' time sniffing her way outside this morning. Even more time getting back in the house. She is uber diligent about her sniffing. Enter the deep water ...

If Bella takes 15 minutes, first thing in the morning in sub-zero temperatures, to sniff her way back into the house, searching for anything that might be trapped under the snow and ice, how much more fervent is our Lord and Savior in searching for us? How much time and under how much dirty, filthy, nasty stuff will He look for us? I mean, we have three dogs. And it's winter. In Alaska. That's a lot of sub-zero cold and nastiness that our sweet Bella sniffs through to come back inside.

Imagine. God loves us enough to look for us in the most revolting of places. Underneath any and all our yuck. I am amazed. Encouraged.

> *"Where can I go from Your Spirit? Or where can I flee from Your presence? If I ascend into heaven, You are there; if I make my bed in hell, behold, You are there. If I take the wings of the morning, and dwell in the uttermost parts of the sea, even there, Your hand shall lead me, and Your right hand shall hold me."*
>
> **Psalm 139:7-10, NKJV**

COURSE CORRECTION

It's a plain ol' latte in a new Alaska mug and slow cool mornings and my mother-in-law's words kind of deep water.

"I will never ..."

I'm pretty certain we've all uttered those words. I know I have. I also know, as my mother-in-law was so apt to say, "Jacquelynn, words were made to be eaten."

Pre-Alaska: "I will never wear plaid flannel." "I will never wear those brown rubber boots."

Six weeks into my Alaskan dream: plaid flannel in the closet and the most awesome Salmon Sisters Xtratufs on my feet.

Deep water reality check. What do you think Saul said about those crazy Jesus followers? His actions speak very clearly about what he thought as he hunted them down and persecuted them.

And then God. And blindness. And sight.

Saul became Paul, and Paul saw. It went against everything he "knew." But now he SAW. And everything else followed. He did an about-face. An epic course correction.

Let me encourage you. God not only allows for course correction; He encourages it.

PEACE IN THE NOISE

It's an ice water in the pink Stanley and—finally—no winter robe to start the day and having the Mac home happiness beyond words.

The cicadas are relentless this year.

Their sound is louder than I remember, and impossible to ignore. It's the kind of noise that makes you want to shut the windows and escape indoors.

Rather than hide indoors this morning, I stayed on the porch with my coffee and let the sound surround me. And somewhere between the buzzing and the breeze, I felt it. Peace. Not because the noise stopped, but because I did.

Deep water message of the day: peace isn't always found in silence. Sometimes it's discovered within the noise—when we stop fighting it, and start listening for the rhythm of grace underneath it all.

The world may be loud, but God still meets us right in the middle of it.

> *"Now may the Lord of peace Himself give you peace at all times and in every way. The Lord be with all of you."*
>
> **2 Thessalonians 3:16, NIV**

SUNDAY, SUNDAY

It's a bottled bubbly water and a much-needed Sunday routine and stillness in the deep water.

Mass was quiet this morning. Actually, it wasn't. The music was fast-paced, and the sanctuary full, but we were all—our family—in a space of quiet. We are huddled these days.

The newborn behind us caught our attention. Her delicate size and soft cooing added to the quiet. Brunch after Mass wasn't the typical meal out. We came home, made a fire, cooked together.

Now, naps are happening. Homework is happening. Reading is happening. We are doing, but in a space of quiet effort and contemplation.

How is it possible to overlook this joy? How often do we miss God's quiet moments? If this is a small reward for seeking Him, how blessed will those who seek Him and find Him be?

> *"And you will seek Me and find Me, when you search for Me with all your heart."*
> **Jeremiah 29:13, NKJV**

MANNA IN THE DESERT

It's espresso with cashew milk and coconut sugar and humidity-driven curly hair craziness and sigh-filled deep water.

I love food. Total, definitive foodie. Love to eat it, prepare it, read about it, watch others prepare it, watch others eat it (holy heck, mukbang)! In short, food is my thing. Mmmmm. Food.

The truth about food and me? Food makes me sick. Literally. After months and months of pain and discomfort and, at times, disability, we finally learned that my body doesn't like to process food. Food has become my nemesis.

Two-by-four to the forehead deep water this morning. I am part of a bigger trend that elevates food to an unhealthy and unholy status. Food was never meant to be more than just fuel. It exists to sustain us. It exists to provide an opportunity for experiencing community. It exists as part of worship. It does not exist to be an idol. It does not exist to be love. It does not exist to replace or, more specifically, supersede God.

As I wade through the maze of finding what my body can eat to live, I am reminded that God provided manna (which was sufficient sustenance), and God provides Himself (which is sufficient for everything else in life). I need not fear, for He is with me. He will feed me.

Whatever you are putting above God, I wonder what impact it's having on your body.

"No other gods, only Me."

Exodus 20:3, MSG

The Character of God

A RIVER RUNS THROUGH IT

It's espresso with almond milk and coconut sugar in the familiar Miami mug and a break from the extreme heat and changing deep water.

This morning, images of a river fill the space. The beauty of a wide space, a river at peace, flowing silently under a smooth surface. Counter that with the invigorating torrent of a Cat 5 river—rocky and tumultuous. Both rivers. Both flowing. Both moving with purpose.

The deep water reveals the analogy of the river and life. The times of quiet and calm. The days, weeks, even months of torrent and upheaval. The truth of it is life is a river—ever flowing, changing with the seasons. No matter where you are on the river, no matter the category of ups and downs, twists and turns, the river flows. It is teeming with life.

Isn't God so amazing to keep us moving? We progress at different rates throughout, bending and flexing with the challenges all around us. Sometimes riding the rapids, sometimes we float on a sea of glass. Always we relish in the quiet peace.

May He be always glorified no matter the movement of the water.

SQUAWK BOX

It's the last coffee in the speckled mug and the last sunrise on the lake and wishing for the fluffy winter robe to chase away the morning chill.

Mornings at the lake have been glorious. Still water. Misty breezes. The gentle songs of birds. What a treasure! Until yesterday.

Yesterday, the birdsong was interrupted by the most harsh squawking. A friend standing near me offered that I pray for the creature. I countered I'd more likely pray for its demise.

This morning the deep water came courtesy of the screeching bird in question. Why, I wondered, must my last morning here be ruined by this bad bird?!?! And then this bird, this interminable bird, landed in the birch tree not 10 feet from me.

Guess what? It was the most glorious red-headed woodpecker I've seen. And his mate. Simply magnificent creatures. The lesson was easy—never judge a book by its cover (or its squawking).

God's gifts come. We need only put our judgment away to see them.

WAITING FOR THE STORM TO PASS

It's a Pimm's cup and another day of fog and rain and singular deep water.

The deer run in the meadow. They always come in groups, most often a doe and two fawns. We have become joyfully familiar with them.

This morning, there was a singular yearling grazing on the fallen mulberries. This deer was alone. It was a gift to share our mulberries, but the deer's singular status was of note.

Fast forward to the thunder-filled afternoon, storm-led twilight. The dogs needed to go outside before the storm. They were unsettled. Their barking was unusual. They simply would not stop. When I finally went out to them, I realized they were alerting me to the presence of – A SINGULAR DEER. The poor thing was alone. In the meadow. In the midst of thunder and impending storms.

My heart filled with maternal concern. The poor deer. The poor deer, all alone and with storms looming. I rushed to the little. "The deer is all alone in the meadow. It is all alone. And the storms …"

And then the deep water … Aren't we all like the deer? Aren't we all alone, waiting for the storm to pass? God is so good to remind me we are never alone. Not in the meadow. Not in the storm.

> *"I'll never let you down, never walk off and leave you …"*
> **Hebrews 13:5, MSG**

COUNTER-CULTURAL

It's a dragon's milk in a proper beer glass and a day of reaping and resting and deep water full of forethought.

Have you considered …? The father saw the prodigal son while he was still a long way off. That means the father was actively looking for his son. Looking ardently, even from a distance.

Contrary to ancient culture, the father ran to the son. In ancient times, a father would not run. It just wasn't done. This act of the father running and hurrying to his son went against the culture. In fact, running would have been a shameful endeavor. In doing so, the father preemptively assumed shame so his son would not have to.

Lastly, the father had the fatted calf prepared to celebrate the return of the son. The fatted calf was typically set aside for the Passover meal. It could have additionally been prepared for an anticipated feast, but certainly not a feast to celebrate the return of a prodigal.

The fact this father so loved his rebellious son that he watched for him, then ran to him, and celebrated his return as if triumphant is remarkable. It isn't just a lesson for the Pharisees and Sadducees. It's a lesson for all of us.

We have a Father who loves us so dearly that He is willing to forego custom and culture, put aside convention, and make gross exceptions to the rule—no matter our choices or our behavior—simply to rejoice in our return. He awaits our coming. He watches for us. He is prepared to celebrate, no matter the day or hour.

Simply amazing.

> *"The Lord your God in your midst, the Mighty One, will save; He will rejoice over you with gladness, He will quiet you with His love, He will rejoice over you with singing."*
>
> **Zephaniah 3:17, NKJV**

THE IMITATION GAME

It's another day of coffee made by dear friends and finding my tribe and swimming slowly through the deep water.

The only thing Christ asks us to imitate is His humility.

Now there's some deep water.

THE GOSPEL TRUTH

It's an almond milk latte in the Seghesio mug and girls' weekend excitement and childhood memories pulling me down into the deep water.

How many of us grew up in religion? Religion sounds good—it might even look good, but it's not. Religion is a man thing, not a God thing. Whenever we become more focused on things—doing the right thing, saying the right thing, not doing the bad things—we move into religion. Hang your hat there long enough, and you are certain to gain some battle scars.

I grew up in a very faithful family. My struggle was that I only got the religion. I didn't get the gospel. I didn't get grace. I can still remember the reverend shouting from the pulpit about how bad we all were and how we certainly were going to hell if we messed up. That message was woven into the very fabric of my being. God, for me, was all about performing well enough to maybe possibly avoid hell.

Oh, what a sad message.

I'm here to tell you—God is love. God is grace. And forgiveness. And mercy. God wants us to trust Him enough to share when we mess up and to seek Him for comfort and loving correction. He wants us to feel the loving hand of forgiveness and hope.

May you know the boundless, unending love of God.

> **Religion:** *"I messed up. Dad is gonna kill me."*
>
> **Gospel:** *"I messed up. I need to call Dad."*
>
> *"But because of His great love for us, God, who is rich in mercy, made us alive with Christ even when we were dead in transgressions—it is by grace you have been saved. And God raised us up with Christ and seated us with Him in the heavenly realms in Christ Jesus."*
>
> **Ephesians 2:4-6, NIV**

S.T.A.T.

It's an almond milk latte in a mug I can't recall and looking forward and Spirit-filled yoga.

This morning was new. A new way. A new beginning. I went to Holy Yoga. And the infinitely brilliant deep water surrounded me.

Purpose.

Urgency.

One of God. One not. I've lived most of my life with urgency. Performing tends to put you on that track. Go. Go. Go. Now. Now. Now. Oh, the overwhelming sense of urgency in this life.

Purpose lives in the opposite direction. Purpose requires thoughtful action. Timely reflection. In today's yoga class, I forced myself to sit with purpose. The instructor led with Psalm 20. She read it over and over. In the middle of resting in the pain, breathing through the stretch, she reminded us that urgency is in us. Patience and peace are in God. Breathe through the pain, the stretch. Wait on the Lord. It is good. He will not keep you waiting without His purpose.

Breathe on us, oh, breath of God.

> *"May supernatural help be sent from His sanctuary ... Pause in His presence."*
>
> **Psalm 20: 2-3, TPT**

STOP THAT! BAD DOG!

It's a keto coffee in the pretty pink mug and the pretty pink winter robe and prodigal deep water.

It's a rhyme from childhood that expands into adulthood: "It's not so much what you say, but in the way you say. It's not so much the words you choose, but in the way you convey it."

Sometimes, we behave like the crazy Cajun, Doug the dog. Sometimes, we need to be told to stop what we're doing or turn around from bad choices and return home. Sometimes, we are emotional, mental, physical, and spiritual prodigals, running on our own agenda and disregarding the safety of a loving home. Oftentimes, it's just letting our renegade thoughts and emotions run off our tongues, disregarding the "stop that" and "get back here" our hearts know as good boundaries.

The good news is that God knows all about running amok. And while He will offer a stern and loving, "Stop that," He's immeasurably quick to extend welcoming arms of forgiveness. He extends grace and mercy to even the harshest of tongues, the strongest of rogue personal agendas.

> *"I am leaving you with a gift—peace of mind and heart. And the peace I give is a gift the world cannot give. So don't be troubled or afraid."*
>
> **John 14:27, NLT**

THE SUN AND THE MOON AND THE STARS IN THE SKY

It's a cuppa London Fog in the "J" teacup and a morning of solitude and wonder and deep water filled with the sun and the moon and the stars.

I prayed with him. I hugged him. I wished him a good day and sent him into the dark morning to begin his day.

"Go out back and look at the stars," he texted only moments after he'd left me.

And, oh, what a glory-filled sky there was to behold. The little is acutely aware of God's handiwork. He shares that love with his momma. We, the little and I, began our day praising the Father.

> *"Praise Him, sun and moon, praise Him, all you shining stars!"*
>
> **Psalm 148:3, ESV**

But God wasn't finished with me yet ...

Doug the dog and I ventured out for an early morning walk. Bundled up against the cold, I was focused more on getting the walk in than my surroundings. As we came upon the meadow where Doug romps like a gazelle, the morning sun came up and shone upon a frost-covered expanse. Doug ran free, and I marveled at the millions of stars shining in the grass, the sunlight turning frost to wonder.

> *"When I look at the night sky and see the work of Your fingers—the moon and the stars You set in place—what are mere mortals that You should think about them, human beings that You should care for them?"*
>
> **Psalm 8:3-4, NLT**

Praise the God of heaven and earth, the sun and moon and stars. Praise Him who cares for me. For you. For all.

GRAB A SWITCH

It's another paper cup morning and loading up and moving out and gosh the deep water.

"If you want to be punished, you will."

God offers us grace. Forgiveness. It's a free gift through Christ. Confess your sins, repent, and you will be forgiven. How beautiful is that?! Crazy, amazingly beautiful. If …

You see, forgiveness from God is freely given. Accepting it is a "whole 'nother thing." It is a great detour the devil puts in front of us. "Yeah, yeah. You are forgiven, but look at what you did/said/didn't do. Look at your sin …"

Believe the lies of the enemy, and you will be punished. You choose to be punished, even though that punishment is self-inflicted, not from God's hand. And punishment and penance are not the same thing. Restoration of your soul resides in God and with God. When we humble ourselves enough to accept His grace and mercy, there is peace and freedom. When we humble ourselves enough to accept forgiveness and walk away from punishing ourselves, we are free to forgive others.

"… forgiving one another, just as God through Christ has forgiven you."

Ephesians 4:32b, NLT

MIRANDA RIGHTS

It's Keto OS/Max Swiss Chocolate in the morning coffee with heavy cream and swimming in the deep water because when there seems to be too much on my plate God throws me in deep...

Law and grace dance together. Perhaps they are the flip sides of a coin? The not-so-little and I have been discussing moral imperatives and grace. Perhaps the most profound and direct lesson I can share with my incredibly reasoned, moral son is the biblical story of the woman caught in adultery...

She was caught. She was guilty. She deserved the consequences of her choice. And yet. Or better still, Jesus.

"Who stands to condemn you?" He asked.

"No one," she replied.

"Then neither do I."

God calls us to live within the boundaries of His protective law, the Commandments. And He leads and covers with grace. Always grace. Live wisely, live rightly, but lead with grace.

NUCLEAR REACTORS

It's bulletproof coffee in the Miami Mom mug and arctic temps in the dark morning.

Confession: I don't do hurt well. I'd like to think I can handle curve balls and someone else's bad mood with grace and dignity. Not so much. At least not all the time. And that hurts. It points out an area where I need some serious growth.

I'm more of a reactor than a responder. That's one of the many things Jesus did amazingly well. He responded rather than reacted. He knew who He was, where He stood in the big, bad world, and He loved. I want to think He lived life so very well because He never had hurts, deep hurts, but that just isn't true. So, I have this great role model, one who knows the deepest of hurts, and still responds in love and truth.

Are you a reactor or a responder?

> *"He has shown you, O man, what is good; and what does the Lord require of you but to do justly, to love mercy, and to walk humbly with your God?"*
>
> **Micah 6:8, NKJV**

THE BARE NECESSITIES

It's a cardamom milk latte in the Miami Mom mug and dogs hunting squirrels and still deep water.

Do you have everything you need? As we prepare to send the big back to Montana, I am waking up extra early. I'm reviewing the "Mom list" of what he might need. As his mother, I want to do my part to make sure he has everything he needs … and there it is. The deep water.

"Give us this day our daily bread." It is the ultimate request of our Heavenly Father. "Lord, give us what we need. Everything we need, every day. Our daily bread."

The prayer covers specifically what we need for this day, but that request is repeated every day. So, God, give us everything we need. Today.

And He is perfect goodness. Nothing less. He will provide for our every need. May we trust in that provision always.

> *"And my God will supply every need of yours according to His riches in glory in Christ Jesus."*
>
> **Philippians 4:19, ESV**

FAITH

Faith is a complex journey, one that often feels like being surrounded by deep water, where the once familiar can become suddenly unsettling, but the unknown can draw us closer to God. From moments of personal reflection to navigating life's challenges, our faith calls us to trust beyond what we can see and feel. When we find ourselves in the depths of uncertainty, we must remember that true faith is not rooted in comfort, but in a relationship with Christ that transcends circumstance.

MIXED MESSAGES

It's ice water and lunch with one of my besties and summer. Hot Texas summer. And oh the deep water...

We've heard of it—Catholic guilt, Presbyterian performance, Lutheran unworthiness.

Here's a question for you: What does your denomination say about you? What messages does your denomination ingrain in you to the point of general understanding by all?

Is that the message Jesus would teach you? Is that the message Jesus would ingrain into your very being?

Denominations are, at their core, an attempt to categorize "subsections" of faith. They are organizational structures that have coalesced around doctrinal interpretations of scripture and common practices. They have their place, but in any and all of them, you can find life and health and strength ... and dogma and distraction and rules.

Whatever denomination you find yourself in—and even non-denominational is a denomination—make sure that where you are, you are experiencing life, being challenged to see your image conformed to His, and your relationship with the Trinity is ever-vibrant and filling you with freedom.

It is for life, after all, that He set us free.

> *"I have come that they may have life, and that they may have it more abundantly."*
>
> **John 10:10b, NKJV**

DO AS YOU'RE TOLD

It's a venti half-caf latte with two pumps of classic syrup in a paper cup and wow! it's a cold wind and it's good for the soul deep water.

"Go get coffee," I heard in my spirit.

Kind of an odd instruction from the Holy Spirit, given we've got great coffee at home.

"Go to Starbucks® and get coffee," the prompt was clear.

"But it's super cold outside, and I've already had a cup of coffee here ..."

"Go to Starbucks®."

This kind of heavenly persistence demands obedience, so I interrupted my not-so-happy morning, got dressed for the day, and went uptown to the local Starbucks®.

"Pay for your coffee and leave the rest of the money for whoever comes after you."

"Oh. This is why Starbucks®. Now I get it."

Why are we commanded to do good works? 1) It is a tangible manifestation of our faith, and 2) It is good for us. Doing good for others leaves us better. It fills our cup. Doing good for others can turn sadness into gratitude and frustration into hope.

> *"Do not neglect to do good and to share what you have, for such sacrifices are pleasing to God."*
>
> **Hebrews 13:16, ESV**

A FIRM FOUNDATION

It's another Nespresso pod and cream in the pretty pink floral mug and humidity hair—day 6—and Ohio is hotter than Texas?! and I am barely holding up in the air conditioning.

Today's deep water is hard. Foundation-shaking hard. And in the midst of foundations shaking and cracking and being torn apart, I am reminded (even encouraged) that God is God. I am grateful that His permissive will is the foundation for our free will. The freedom to choose Him. The freedom to access all that is good and well and holy. The freedom to, well, choose freedom.

When we came into full communion in the Roman Catholic Church, many of our Protestant friends and family had questions. Lots of questions. One of the most personal to me was questioning how a survivor of sexual abuse could ever remotely consider joining a church where similar abuses have happened. "How, Jackie, how?!" so many pleaded.

Fast forward to today.

Friends. Abuse is not singular to one person, or one church, or one denomination. Abuse exists everywhere. It has existed for as long as evil has been loose on the earth, but I want to encourage you: God's grace and mercy are sufficient. Healing and freedom are possible for survivors.

I know this because I've walked it out.

The behavior of one man does not invalidate God's mission in and for the church. The choices of broken, sinful men do not wipe out His goodness nor the goodness of His church. Because, dear ones, God works in the midst of sin and brokenness every single day. There will continue to be exposures and new revelations of evil at work in places where evil should never be permitted to work, and while each time we hear of something new, it is daunting and heartbreaking, it is not the end of things. When men (and women) of the church choose to sin, it does not invalidate God.

GROWTH OPPORTUNITY

It's an unappealing almond milk latte in the new Hochatown mug and a daily temperature tango and palm fronds for the centerpiece.

As I enter Holy Week, the deep water spotlights a Holy truth:

Our faith is not about making ourselves feel better.

Draw nearer to the love of Christ. Not to make yourself feel better, but to expand and increase your relationship with Him.

GYPSIES, TRAMPS, AND THIEVES

It's a stein of King Street stout and brotherly escapades and settling deep water.

When the Mac and I were fairly newly married, we met with one of our church pastors. A touch base session, two—thanks to the military—veritable strangers trying to come together. Our wise pastor had this to share with us:

"Maybe you are both hard-wired to wander. Maybe you won't be content settling into one place or at least one place for a long time."

Thirty-three moves later, I think Rev. Hilliard may have touched on something. There are souls that look for the next thing before they even stop to enjoy the now thing. I thought I had found "my place," but almost as quickly as I chose it, another move.

Deep water epiphany.

It isn't about a place. It's about a relationship.

Yes, there are those prone to wander. New adventures at every turn kind of explorers. The key is not in the wandering or the places; the key is in the faith. I can travel the world, moving often, and still be settled. It is in my faith where I am at peace. My faith is the foundation that lets me roam free.

> "Now may the Lord of peace Himself give you peace at all times and in every way. The Lord be with you all."
>
> 2 Thessalonians 3:16, NIV

MORE! MORE! MORE!

It's a not-yet-healthy mocha in the new logo mug and a happy-to-be-home busy day and rearranging the furniture so we can sit by the fire season.

More! More! More!

Is there ever enough? Food? Drink? Fun? Stuff? Time? Will there ever be enough? We spend so much of our lives, our thoughts, and our energy striving for "enough" that it often leaves me wondering ... Will there ever be a point where I am satisfied?

Deep water clarity this morning.

No. Nope. Not gonna happen. There will actually never really truly be enough.

Because all the stuff, things, everything we keep reaching for, none of that is what will ultimately satisfy us.

It's our faith that fills us. There, we find enough. More than enough. Not a thing. Not a thought. Not even the endless striving to be "the best version of me I can be."

Relationship. That fills. God. Fills.

BRINGING IT TO THE ALTAR

It's a super hot mocha in the Seghesio mug and stretching out to reach the finish line and denim denim ... and more denim.

The deep water is all about the altar today.

Life requires us to put things on the altar. The altar of forgiveness. The altar of faith. The altar of love. There is a giving up, a sacrificing, in the ebb and flow of a life well lived.

Be purposeful in what you are willing to sacrifice.

> *"Beloved friends, what should be our proper response to God's marvelous mercies? I encourage you to surrender yourselves to God to be His sacred, living sacrifices. And live in holiness, experiencing all the delights of His heart. For this becomes your genuine expression of worship."*
>
> **Romans 12:1, TPT**

TENSION IN THE AIR

It's a sugar-free almond milk nutty Irishman in a paper cup and sun and snow and doing the thing even though it scares you.

This week. Actually, one week from today, is my first book's deadline. It'll be written. And then it's no longer a hypothetical. It'll be "real." And that feels so huge.

The deep water reminds me that the tension between doing what we are called to do and fear is echoed in Christ's progression to the cross. Jesus entered town amidst pomp and circumstance, knowing full well the suffering that would soon be upon Him. Despite very human fear and trepidation, He did the thing anyway.

May God be glorified in all He calls us to do, especially when the thing makes us afraid.

> *"... for the Lord your God is with you wherever you go."*
>
> **Joshua 1:9b, NKJV**

SIGNS AND WONDERS

It's a second glass of Cade in a pinot glass (because smaller portions) and a day of cooking and enjoying and cooking and enjoying some more and winter white tops and bottoms because that's how I roll.

Christmas Eve deep water is all about my daddy.

This morning, amidst baking and baking and anticipating baking tomorrow, the oven started freaking out. Lights flashing. Alarms ringing. It was quite the mess. "Dad, if you could offer some assistance (as an intercessor) and help us out with this oven, I'd greatly appreciate it."

The oven is fine.

Fast forward to heavy appetizers and the Christmas Eve homily. Long and short of it, Fr. Dan offers, "You never know how much God is all you need until God is all you have." That is something my dad said. Often.

For the first time since he died, today was the day I protested. "No!" Today was the first time I really resented his absence. Today has been hard. In the midst of it, whether lightheartedly asking him to help with the oven, or more seriously hearing his echo in the priest's words, my dad is with us.

Hoping your Christmas Eve is filled.

UNPREPARED

It's a really really large oat milk latte in a paper cup and running on empty and the deep water.

Unprepared. Not a typical method for living life. We have schedules and planners. To-do lists and unlimited, technology-driven reminders. Calendar apps. You get the idea. Unprepared is not being a good Scout.

10:52 PM Alaska Standard Time put me face-to-face, literally, with the blessing of being unprepared. A moose. Larger than life. Actually, as large as real life, but huge. Makes me wonder … Was anyone really prepared for Jesus?

They anticipated. They thought they'd prepared. They kept to their schedules. Adhered to the Law (or not). And they prepared. It was only when they set down their preparedness that they could see the Savior. Only when they were unprepared did they see the blessing.

Enjoying the view from my window—entirely unprepared.

ITSY BITSY, TEENIE WEENIE

It's a second oat milk latte in the "because adulting is hard" mug and birdsong and holding patterns.

The deep water is vast, but today's is all about the most minute of things. What shouts at you? What in life is big and bold enough to command your attention? Demand your time?

Flip that coin.

What is seemingly (or literally) so small you only see it when everything else has been done? Is that thing really the least important? Maybe it is. Good for you prioritizing and accomplishing. But if the smallest thing is only small because either you don't like it, it's difficult, it's not popular, or … you get the idea, then maybe it's time to increase the point size or choose a more noticeable font. You know, reprioritize.

Faith like a tiny mustard seed—sometimes, the most minute IS the most important.

FAITH OVER COMFORT

It's coffee with half and half in the worn Miami mug and the pretty pink summer robe and eat-some-bananas leg cramps to start the day.

What's your routine? You know, the things you do because they provide comfortable structure to your life. It's Sunday, so what is your Sunday routine? Coffee and some smooth jazz? Pop Tarts for the kids on the way to church? A long training ride with your Peloton group?

This morning's deep water came in the form of a question: What do you avoid because the routine of it is uncomfortable, even intimidating?

All too often, I hear people say they avoid church, the Catholic church in particular, because they don't know "the routine." The idea of going to a church where everyone else knows what to do and when and you don't feels too difficult. Uncomfortable. It certainly doesn't feel welcoming.

Why is it we are more than ready to ask questions about politics, sports, the latest diet fad, but not our faith (or the potential of a faith)? Why is it we are willing to be uncomfortable almost anywhere but in church?

TO TELL THE TRUTH

It's a Mac-made almond milk latte in the pretty Poland mug and a bed full of dogs and before my feet hit the floor deep water.

The Mac. My Mac. He makes me coffee most mornings. It is an act of love and an act of selfless service. (He doesn't even drink coffee.) It endears my Mac to me with great significance. He is super crazy busy this morning and yet, despite my insistence that he is too busy, away he went. He returned with my coffee in hand and a lovely morning greeting and a kiss.

And as he walked away, my gut was filled with frustration. My mind actually did a 180° and went from, "Gosh. Am I ever so blessed?" to someone else's thoughts: "Is he really doing this because he loves you or just to appease you so he can move on with his day?"

Let me tell you. My Mac is thoughtful. He is generous. He adores me. Bringing me coffee is a genuine act. I know this! And yet ...

The devil will find a way. He will do his utmost to kill love. Satan, in the words of my bestie, "is an a&$!"

This morning's deep water is a reminder.

> "The thief comes only to kill, steal, and destroy."
>
> **John 10:10a, NIV**

Live in love.

WE ARE FAMILY

It's an extra-large almond milk latte in the new Warsaw mug and the pretty pink floral winter robe and a day of preparation.

This week has been all about preparing. Readying the rooms of the boy and the not-so-little middle for their return. Shopping in preparation for feeding them. Shopping to feed the entire family for Thanksgiving. Cleaning in preparation for Thanksgiving week. Yard work to clean up the autumn leaves. A lot of preparation.

All in anticipation of being together.

And then the deep water ... If we are this diligent to prepare a place for our family, how much more prepared is God in anticipation of His children?

> *"And if I go and prepare a place for you, I will come again and receive you to Myself; that where I am, there you may be also."*
>
> **John 14:3, NKJV**

Happy preparing.

BUILDING BRIDGES

It's an early start to the day (thanks Doug the dog) and an airport latte and the deep water.

Jesus is our High Priest. He alone has the power to forgive our sins. So why confession? To a priest? To another? Why share the bad things, the shameful things, the guilt?

Because "As long as you are guilty, your soul will cry for punishment" (Unknown).

We share because it brings healing. Accountability. An avenue for justice.

Our souls require forgiveness, our sins washed clean in the cleansing flow. Our souls also inherently seek justice and healing. Confession is the bridge to both.

> "Therefore, confess your sins to each other and pray for each other so that you may be healed."
>
> **James 5:16a, NIV**

> "If we confess our sins, He is faithful and just and will forgive us our sins and purify us from all unrighteousness."
>
> **1 John 1:9, NIV**

A STRANGER IN A STRANGE LAND

It's a water bottle and a noisy room heater and shockingly cold Ohio weather for this Texas girl.

I don't sleep well in hotels. Unfamiliar spaces and noises, smells, and lights. Honestly, I find it hard to rest. Hmmm ... the deep water. I don't rest in places I don't know.

Maybe that's why Jesus told us to get to know Him.

As a Christ follower, each of us has access to the "peace that passes all understanding." We have access to it. It is part of God's free gift to us through Jesus. That said, if we aren't familiar with God, we won't know what God's peace looks like, feels like, etc.

Reading the Bible—routinely—gives us the best method for getting to know God. As we get to know Him, we will become familiar with Him. And, as the saying goes, familiarity breeds contentment. Personally, I love the idea of being content in the Father. Basking in His peace. Even in—especially in—unfamiliar places.

> *"That I may know Him and the power of His resurrection ..."*
> **Philippians 3:10, ESV**

THEY WILL KNOW WE ARE CHRISTIANS

It's a healthy mocha in the Texas mug and not PC deep water.

"You're a Redskin," said the man passing us in the grocery store parking lot. It took a second for me to realize A) he was talking to me, and B) he had identified me as part of something larger.

I am a Redskin. So is the Mac. William is a Redhawk. We are all part of the larger group known as Miamians. Graduates of Miami University. Love and honor and all that means. Time has changed the mascot, but not the institution.

That got me thinking: how has time changed the names of Christians? How does that limit us? Increase us? Have the name changes influenced the greater institution of Christianity? Have the name changes influenced us as individuals? Who are you? How do others know? Are you part of something larger, easily recognized, and calling out to others as they pass you in the parking lot?

> "By this all will know that You are My disciples, if you have love for one another."
>
> **John 13:35, NKJV**

WHAT'S YOUR CREDIT SCORE?

It's Donut Shop coffee in the Miami Mom mug and an early start to a busy day.

"God knows because He's God. The devil knows because he's old."

A dear friend shared this quote with me last night. I joked I'd have to post it on my Facebook page. And then I promptly recanted. You just can't force God to give you some amazing revelation. But being God, He never disappoints, so here ya' go ...

Most of us give God the credit for being God. But how often do we give the devil equal credit? First and foremost, the devil is NOT GOD. Stop giving him the power of God. The importance of God. The influence of God. What he, the devil, deserves is the respect due to the long-lived.

It is the wisdom of age and experience that equips the devil with his knowledge and skill, not omnipotence. It is the wisdom of age and experience that gives the devil the insight, almost shocking insight, into our lives. He's seen someone like us before, and he knows how to deal with that particular challenge, weakness, instability, etc. He also knows how to knock out even the smallest bit of our God-given strength. It is the wisdom of age and experience that makes the devil such a formidable enemy.

And, as in life, age and wisdom deserve our utmost respect. In the case of Satan, a healthy respect in the way you respect that a poisonous snake can bite you and cause you harm. Respect is not worship. Respect is not obedience. Respect is not agreement, or complicity, or acceptance. We would be wise to recognize the age and experience and knowledge accumulated by the devil. He probably even knows the Bible better than us. So, we can give him his due. And we must never, for even the slightest fraction of a second, underestimate what he has in his bag of tricks.

That said, Christians have something the devil does not. We have access to the Victor. We have the ability to defeat the cunning, old devil's schemes and plans and tiny, itsy-bitsy attempts to derail our lives. The devil is so good at his job that he often makes it easy for us to forget he is ultimately the loser. Perhaps this is why the Bible tells us to take every thought captive and hold it up to the truth of the Word of God. If we begin where we are most vulnerable—our thoughts—the devil doesn't stand a chance. We can defeat him before he begins. Wisdom and experience be damned, Satan.

We've got God. The strength of God. The unlimited resources of God. The mind of God.

And He wins.

Every time!

> *"But thanks be to God! He gives us the victory through our Lord Jesus Christ."*
>
> **1 Corinthians 15:57, NIV**

WHAT'S IN THE FRIDGE?

It's a leftover mocha in the Netherlands mug and cozy layers because seasons and deep water.

It's a leftover kind of night … Leftover dinner, leftover wine, leftover tasks from earlier this week that might just have to wait until tomorrow.

So often, it seems we are running around banking on leftovers. I'm not sure that's really the life God envisioned for us. His Word promises provision for all time. Jesus's sacrifice wasn't just something that we could pull from yesterday as leftovers for today. It is an active, ongoing, for today and tomorrow and always kind of faith. We don't have to rely on yesterday's leftovers.

That's one of the great beauties of being a Christian. God has provided exceedingly abundantly more than we could ever hope or imagine, and it just keeps accumulating. There are no leftovers. And that is a beautiful thing.

> *"Behold, I am doing a new thing; now it springs forth, do you not perceive it?"*
>
> **Isaiah 43:19a, ESV**

NIGHT MOVES

It's the Miami mug and summer quiet and the deep water courtesy of God and the Channel 5 News.

Thieves are rendering DFW dark. They're stealing the copper wire from highway lights and leaving major roadways dark and, as a result, difficult to navigate. Sometimes, things are even hazardous.

Satan acts in the same manner in our lives. He does his best to steal our light. He acts in darkness, setting the stage for us to stumble, get lost, and live in hazardous conditions.

What an opportunity to know the thief is out there and to know God has already given us everything we need to combat his darkness and live in the light.

> *"But if we walk in the light, as He is in the light, we have fellowship with one another, and the blood of Jesus His Son cleanses us from all sin."*
>
> 1 John 1:7, ESV

CRYSTAL CLEAR

Sunrise today is well ordinary. I'm wrapped in the Red's blanket. Almond/coconut milk latte to drink.

Today's deep water is all about the sunrise. The ordinary, oh it's there again, but not exceptionally beautiful or noteworthy sunrise. The community, friends, and family of Jesus felt the same way about Him.

> *Then they scoffed, "He's just the carpenter's son, and we know Mary, his mother, and his brothers--James, Joseph, Simon, and Judas."*
>
> **Matthew 13:55-56a, NLT**

When we become so completely familiar with someone or something, it's all too easy to miss the beauty right in front of us. The majesty of a sunrise. The glory of our Savior.

Behold the extraordinary contained in the familiar.

MONSTERS UNDER THE BED

It's a second latte in the now unrecognizable Miami mug and exorcising demons and deep water on the way to school.

The little needed to go in early today and wanted two of the dogs to ride along—because car rides. At the first stop light, we stopped next to a plumbing truck with a larger-than-life boy on the side. Doug the dog was not impressed. In fact, he began to growl and then to bark. Alliyah joined in. Neither of them was going to let that big, bad boy get us. They would fight the good fight of protection on our behalf.

Then, the deep water.

How many times do we see enemies where there are none? In others? In ourselves?

> *"For we are not fighting against flesh-and-blood enemies, but against evil rulers and authorities of the unseen world, against mighty powers in this dark world, and against evil spirits in the heavenly places."*
>
> **Ephesians 6:12, NLT**

IGNORANCE ISN'T BLISS

It's a venti latte in the all-too-familiar paper cup and humbling moments and a 10-foot platform dive straight into the deep water...

"If you only love those that love you back, what kind of love is that?"

All those gushy, Hollywood moments. Are those really love? I mean, it sounds nice, it feels nice, it looks nice, but love???

Jesus loved Judas.

He chose him as one of His closest friends and disciples. He knew Judas would betray Him—from the beginning—and yet, He called him friend and loved him still. Washed his feet, y'all! When Judas kissed Jesus in the ultimate act of betrayal, Jesus asked God to forgive him. Because Judas really, truly didn't know what he was doing or the consequences of his actions.

> *"But God demonstrates His own love toward us, in that while we were still sinners, Christ died for us."*
>
> **Romans 5:8, NKJV**

THE FLIP
SIDE OF THE COIN

It's a dark chocolate hot cocoa and open windows fresh air and the peace of having the Mac home.

Stop. Look left. Look right. Don't miss it deep water today.

Jesus lived and died as the sacrifice for all our sins. He took the punishment for our crimes. And that is sufficient unto the day.

But that's not the whole story.

You see. It's not just paying the price for us. And I, for one, have missed this other part of the equation. Until now.

It's the forgiveness and how we feel about it.

We aren't meant to suffer the shame of our sin once we are forgiven. The devil is a sly little bugger, isn't he? Jesus forgives us, but the devil still torments us with the shame of the crime.

Great news! The best news! We have the opportunity to be forgiven and jettison the shame as well. Be gone, thoughts!

The deep water is encouraging. Confession. Reconciliation. Forgiveness. And the peace that passes all understanding.

Shame is out. Freedom is in.

> *"There is therefore now no condemnation to those who are in Christ Jesus, who do not walk according to the flesh, but according to the Spirit."*
>
> **Romans 8:1, NKJV**

GO TEAM!

It's the last of the coffee in this year's pink tulip mug and settling into the almost empty nest routine and people and party-planning-filled days.

The deep water is for all the athletes in the house.

    Why do you kneel at Mass?

    When your coach talks, you take a knee.

    Mic drop.

> "Come, let us worship and bow down. Let us kneel before the Lord, our maker, for he is our God."
>
> **Psalm 95:6, NLT**

VIRTUE

Virtue is often misunderstood—sometimes appearing as something rigid, unattainable, or even burdensome. But what if virtue isn't about restriction but rather about freedom? What if it is about seeing things clearly and choosing what is truly good rather than what simply looks or feels appealing? Much like the honeysuckle's deceptive beauty or the color-coordinated duvet cover that hides the dirt, virtue calls us beyond surface-level appearances to something deeper, richer, and ultimately life-giving.

A ROSE BY ANY OTHER NAME

It's an LMNT water in the pink Stanley and dog park happiness and planting all the spring and summer pots.

I was carrying the herbs and flowers from the back of the Jeep around to the back deck. The sweet and intoxicating smell of honeysuckle danced around me. The blossoms were beautiful in their yellow and white gowns. It was compelling. Compelling enough to stop me from the task at hand.

Hello, deep water.

These gorgeous bushes. They fill the ground cover space around the entirety of the forest and clothe the perimeter of our yard. I love how they look! I love how they smell! But they are invasive!

What a contrast. Something that looks and smells so lovely is deadly. Honeysuckle will take over and drown out all the natural beauty that occurs in the space around it. Nothing good or natural can thrive next to it. It kind of makes me think of the devil. How many instances in our lives do things look and smell and seem entirely wonderful and lovely only to be proven deadly? How often does Satan use what appears excellent to be terminal?

> *"No wonder, for even Satan disguises himself as an angel of light."*
>
> **2 Corinthians 11:14, NASB**

HIDING IN PLAIN SIGHT

It's a hazelnut coffee with cream in the new Romania mug and opening the windows sleeping and graduation preparation excitement.

So, I'm making the bed this morning with the new Scandinavian method comforters (yeah, that's a story. But it's for another day). As I work, insight floods my thoughts. Today's deep water is courtesy of Jesus and the Oma and IKEA.

To what lengths will we go to cover up our dirt?

Yesterday, I was at IKEA trying to select new comforters and duvet covers. There were lots of choices, and if you know me at all, I need to make the best choice to create the warm, cosy environment that we call home. Because she is an awesome partner in crime, I FaceTime the Oma.

"Which of these duvet covers do you think would work best?" I ask.

I offered up three options, one of which included a white duvet cover. All of our bedding is white, so a white duvet cover would seem to be a good choice.

"Well, you have dogs … and they get on the bed … so I'm not thinking white is the best option. Dirty paws and all."

Ultimately, I purchased several options, including the white one. I brought them home, and had another FaceTime call with the Oma and the choices in the space to confirm colors and such. We didn't choose the white. Because dogs. And here enters this morning's deep water…

To what extent will you go to cover up your dirt? The green duvet covers hide the dirt. And, with dogs that are allowed on the bed, there will be dirt. That is a given. But we don't want to look at it. We don't want that dirt to ruin the beauty that we see. God forbid we present something that is less than clean … and beautiful … and perfect.

Today I'm wondering how often I try to cover up the dirt within me. And in how many and what ways do I try to disguise that which is less than clean and beautiful?

This morning started far too early, and the task list was overwhelmingly long. Truth be told, I was acting in all sorts of ways that were anything but beautiful. No hiding from it. Because dirt isn't always literal. Spiritual dirt is anything but. I think this is the point of confession. Recognizing and taking ownership of the dirt we are trying to cover up and putting it in a place where it can be seen and healed and forgiven.

Maybe that is why He clothes us in pristine, spotless white garments—so no dirt can hide.

> "... that He may sanctify and cleanse her with the washing of water by the Word, that He might present her to Himself a glorious church, not having spot or wrinkle or any such thing, but that she should be holy and without blemish."
>
> **Ephesians 5:26-27, NKJV**

THE ULTIMATE PREPPER

It's a two-cup of coffee kind of morning. Rainy day number three. And the robe has been swapped for a raincoat.

Today's deep water is all about planning. Planning and preparing. It occurred to me I put a lot of time and effort into planning and preparing. Planning meals. Preparing meals. Planning the family calendar. Preparing for sporting events. Planning and preparing for Mac's travel. My travel. Family travel. It's a chunk of my day. Every day.

God is a planner as well.

> *"For I know the plans I have for you," declares the Lord, "plans to prosper you and not to harm you, plans to give you hope and a future."*
>
> **Jeremiah 29:11, NIV**

And God prepares … God has prepared.

> *"What no eye has seen, what no ear has heard, and what no human mind has conceived"—the things God has prepared for those who love him—*
>
> **1 Corinthians 2:8-10, NIV**

I spend so much of my time planning and preparing. God plans. God prepares. I wonder, How much time do I spend planning and preparing for my heavenly future? Planning and preparing for my day? For this day, as a Christ follower?

LETTING IT ALL HANG OUT

The rosé has been drunk and the Oma and Opa have departed the pattern and FaceBook reminded me of some long-forgotten deep water.

"It's just us girls" seems to be a freeing sentiment. The ability to relax, let your hair down and just be. It seems freeing. Until the talking starts. The husband-bashing, the life's-just-not-fair, and oh, can-I-just-tell-you laments ...

I went on a girls' weekend once. It was an opportunity, and I was grateful. And then the talking started. And my impressions of these women changed. My impressions of their husbands, most of whom I did not know, changed. I changed.

It's not freeing to "let your hair down" and malign another. Especially your husband. It is anything but freeing. It is bondage at its deepest and most basic level. I'm not talking about seeking honest, Christ-centered help from a trusted sister in Christ here. I'm talking about the bad-mouthing and complaining so many women feel entitled to in the company of "just us girls." It swiftly becomes a badge of honor to top one another with who has it the worst or who must put up with the most. Exaggerated. Self-serving. Family-shredding garbage.

Ladies. Stop it. A lady shouldn't act in such a manner. A daughter of the King wouldn't act in such a manner. You have the power of life and death in you. Speak life.

> *"Wives, understand and support your husbands in ways that show your support for Christ."*
>
> **Ephesians 5:22, MSG**

HUSH, CHATTY MONKEY!

It's the routine mocha in the Homestead mug and yep still in the 30s to start the day.

I don't want to hear it.

Seriously.

Unless it is a very real problem with which you need help, I don't want to hear all about how hard or miserable or terrible life is. If I can do something for you to help you, bring it on—no filter, no hesitation. Otherwise, how do I say this nicely???

Misery loves company. But that kind of company isn't life-giving. Miserable company just makes everyone more comfortable in their misery.

Speak life.

> *"Let no corrupting talk come out of your mouths, but only such as is good for building up, as fits the occasion, that it may give grace to those who hear."*
>
> **Ephesians 4:29, ESV**

YOU WANNA GO?!

It's an anticipated date night cocktail and enjoying the last days of summer sun and U of M deep water.

> "Competitive but not combative."
>
> **Coach Harbaugh**

When did competing mean fighting? When did we move from challenging one another to hurting one another?

The deep water cautions me. Engaging another does not have to mean enraging another.

> "So then, let us pursue what makes for peace and for mutual upbuilding."
>
> **Romans 14:19, ESV**

THE THEORY OF RELATIVITY

Sunrise today is the dull hazy orange of summer. I'm wrapped in the Mac's Bengals sweatshirt and it's sweet spiced Nana mint tea to drink.

Today began with a so-not-PC deep water lesson. The Collect from my morning devotion put it right out there. "... In all we do, direct us to the fulfilling of Your purpose." In ALL we do. So very black and white. Not the hesitant, I-can-talk-my-way-around-it attitude so popular today. There is no relativism here. All. Everything.

Likewise, there is action. In all we DO. An action verb. God expects us; God equips us to do. We are to be in Him, and in being, we are compelled to do. Christ was in God and with God, and Christ did the Father's will. Action. All for the Heavenly Father's purpose.

As a wise man once said, "Do or do not. There is no try."

Yoda got it right. And we are called to do it all for the glory of the Father.

CONSTRUCTION ZONE AHEAD

It's a cardamom latte in the Miami mug and a quick start to a full day and deep water courtesy of the construction on the way to the vet.

Texas roads seem always to be under construction. This morning's drive found me in the middle of road work and several tractor-trailers and work trucks. "This place is always a work in progress." I lamented to the Sheltie. Ugh!

And there it is ... Yes. Always a work in progress. We are the same. Each day is a work of progress toward (or away from) the person God designed us to be. It can be frustrating. How many times do we bemoan learning the "same lesson over again"? How many times do we wish we were finished with the current work in which we find ourselves? How many times???

Thank God, literally, we are always a work in progress. That we have unlimited grace to continue progressing rather than remain where we are.

> *"Being confident of this very thing, that He who has begun a good work in you will complete it until the day of Christ Jesus."*
>
> **Philippians 1:6, NKJV**

CHOICES

It's an extra foamy latte in the Miami mug and no time for anything because ... the deep water!

It started in the Garden of Eden. They had everything good and perfect and from God. And they chose the one bad thing. Presented with unlimited good options, they chose the one bad option. And so it is for the rest of human history.

Presented with what, in this day and age, are seemingly limitless good options, why do so many of us choose poorly? Why do we look at all God has given us that would serve us well and then turn and choose otherwise?

This morning's message is brought to you by Doug the dog. Doug has four bowls of water, two bones, and five toys available to him. He chooses to drink out of the toilet, grab the new cup holder off the counter, and drag laundry downstairs to me. He clearly has lots of good options and chooses otherwise.

> *"There is a way that seems right to a man, but its end is the way to death."*
>
> **Proverbs 14:12, ESV**

IDENTITY CRISIS

It's a second cup of cardamom French toast tea in the self-steeping glass and putting up literal walls and the favorite sweater to ward off the morning chill.

This week begins the process of eliminating offending foods. I am left without my coffee and my wine … I am not to have anything beyond meat, chicken, fish, and greens. I am left without the things that make me, well, me.

LOL. The deep water. Really? Food is who I am? It feels almost like the rich man and the eye of the needle. Have I really put food and drink that high up on the list of what's important in my life? To give it up feels desperate.

God is so good and loving to remind me that anything we put in front of Him is detrimental. Even life-ending. When we do not love God first, we love Him last, and that is not the path to salvation.

In all things. In all ways. Love the Lord your God with all … you get the picture. What are you putting in front of your love of God today?

STEP UP AND STEP OUT

It's a keto coffee in the William and Mary mug and showing off our alma mater and stepping up.

It's a beautiful sunny morning, and Doug the dog and I ventured out for a walk. Beautiful and sunny … and 10° without a windchill. I can only imagine what it is with the windchill.

Yesterday one of my A-Team, my accountability partner, and I had a talk. It was a beginning-of- the-year-what-goals-are-we-setting kind of conversation. And we both agreed it was time to step it up and step into this new year. Toward the end of the conversation, we agreed to have a "come to Jesus" time of reflection at the end of the day and then with one another each week. We need to get up and get going and we are both taking our time doing it. What better way than to prayerfully bring our goals and ourselves in front of Jesus?

In steps the deep water. My initial thought as I was walking in the bitter cold this morning was that I wanted to do whatever I could to avoid a negative conversation with my friend and partner. I wanted to be accountable, but my initial inclination was to avoid some kind of predetermined punishment, which was not at all what the Lord was asking from me or from us! God isn't asking us to be accountable to Him or to one another or even to ourselves to avoid punishment. He asks us to be reflective so that we can find better ways to walk into truth and life and the abundance He has for us.

As we set out to achieve our goals, let's look for ways to be better, not focus on ways we think we might have failed.

YEAH. MAYBE. NOT REALLY.

It's yesterday's Sodaro and much-needed rain and "damn-straight-skippy" deep water.

If you continue to do the things you say you regret, you don't really regret them. Or at least not enough to change.

So, here's the deep water question for today: If you continue to do things you regret, say you regret or want to change, whom do you value less—yourself or the person and people your actions impact?

Think about it.

> "My lofty desires to do what is good are dashed when I do the things I want to avoid. So if my behavior contradicts my desires to do good, I must conclude that it's not my true identity doing it, but the unwelcome intruder of sin hindering me from who I really am."
>
> **Romans 7:19, TPT**

WILLFUL DISOBEDIENCE

It's a pumpkin cinnamon roll latte in the pink floral mug and enough wind to undo even a news anchor's hair and finding friendship and connection amidst social distancing.

Willful disobedience. Absolutely gets under my skin. Makes me struggle as a parent. Intentionally choosing to do wrong ... Not cool.

Enter Bella. Our beautiful Saint Bernard. My girly girl. In her old age, she's becoming stubborn. Obstinate even. This morning, when I called her to come inside, she looked at me and sat down. Turned around, looked at me, and intentionally sat down and refused to come in.

Deep water time. How often does God reach out to us, call to us, only to have us turn around and sit down? Act in opposition to what he has asked us to do? Willful disobedience. And yet He loves us still.

> *"If you love Me, you will keep My commandments."*
> **John 14:15, ESV**

Ouch.

ALL BY MYSELF

It's Friday! Strongbow on behalf of our friend Norm boys doing what they do and deep water.

"Thou shalt have no other gods before me." One of the Big Ten. There is a lot of talk about not making your spouse your god, your marriage your god, your career your god, your children your god, your diet your god ... and the list goes on and on. Here comes the deep water

Wait for it.

How about not making you your god?

What about "You do you, and I'll do me." Yeah, no. That isn't biblical—not even a little bit. You see, it's not just about countering today's relativist mentality. It's about putting God first. Get out of your own way. It's not about doing what you want to do; it's about doing what God wants you to do. The way He'd have you do it. Every. Single. Time. When what and how and when and where and why are about you—you have become your own god. I don't know about you, but I'm not so sure I want the responsibility that comes with being God.

"... choose for yourselves this day whom you will serve ..."

Joshua 24:15, NKJV

THROWING IN THE TOWEL

It's the next 24 ounces of water in the new TAPS bottle and crisp sunshine and keeping my head above the waves deep water.

When did you give up? Why? Be honest with yourself. Take responsibility for the choice(s). Was it diet? Exercise? What about doing the real work of relationship? Being truthful? When did you stop _____?

If you really look at that choice, there is (was) a reason. "It's too hard," isn't it. At some point you ceased making the good choice, the better choice, because you bailed on you. Now, I'm not talking about letting go when it was the best choice. I'm talking about those times when you walked away from choosing your best.

I've been sitting in a lot of that muck the past few weeks. Tons of deep water acknowledgment and taking ownership of my behavior. My lack of behavior. And it stinks.

I used to_____ is not here. It is not now. And most of those choices could either be 1) resurrected or 2) modified for current circumstances ... if only. If only. I'm learning a lot about motivation and success dynamics. Today's takeaway is the life buoy in the deep water.

Never miss twice.

We all have a bad day. Just make sure you don't carry it over 'til tomorrow. Write your goal as an action item. Give it a date, a time, and a place. All of it. And then get going. When that day comes—the kind of day that sets you back—make sure you don't miss twice.

> *"I'm not saying that I have this all together, that I have it made. But I am well on my way, reaching out for Christ, who has so wondrously reached out for me. Friends, don't get me wrong: By no means do I count myself an expert in all of this, but I've got my eye on the goal, where God is beckoning us onward—to Jesus. I'm off and running, and I'm not turning back."*
>
> **Philippians 3:13-14, MSG**

LIPSTICK ON A PIG

It's a milkadamia macchiato in the monogram mug and time zone sleeplessness and change of seasons decorating.

If you know me or you've been to my house, you'll know that I keep a pretty tidy space. I am the daughter of Jack Wiersma, after all.

I take laundry about as seriously as I take any cleaning endeavor. These are the things we put on our bodies. Clothes need to be clean and fresh. It makes you look better and, personally, I think a nice fresh outfit makes you feel better.

Imagine my absolute shock and dismay when I decided to try laundry stripping of the little's clothes. All of them. Not just the baseball gear. Absolute shock!

Kind of ironic that the deep water rises out of the mud bath that ensued from that endeavor. Got me thinking about how often we make things look clean and pretty when, in actuality, there's hidden dirt and grime and ugliness below the surface. It's the polite Southerner who really is polite for its own sake. It's doing the right thing with a pretty crappy attitude. It's, as my daddy would say, "polishing a turd."

Where are there places in your life that look pretty on the outside but are ugly, nasty, and dirty below the surface?

> *"And now, why do you wait? Rise and be baptized and wash away your sins, calling on His name."*
>
> **Acts 22:16, ESV**

YOUR FAVORITE SINS

It's a post-Mass almond milk latte in a paper cup and breaking the fast with the not-so-little and turning up some tunes with the windows open.

Kenny Chesney. Fun to listen to. Jammin' while cooking. Curveball deep water from a baseball fan artist to a baseball mom.

"It's always your favorite sins that do you in."

Dang! Right between the eyes, that one.

I don't love considering my sinful self. It's kind of ugly. And painful. Add to that the very real experience that we all have "favorite sins," and I just want to tune it all out.

Reality check: anything we put before and/or above God is sin. Which are your favorites?

HAPPY, HAPPY, JOY, JOY

It's a second hazelnut coffee with cream in the favorite pumpkin mug and falling leaves and autumn splendor office views and almost turtleneck season!

The deep water has been sitting for a bit. Lingering and deepening into inky revelation.

God wants us to be happy. Yep. I said it. He actually does really want us to be happy. Eternally celebratory. And therein lies the, perhaps, biggest bait and switch of all.

You see, I have been one staunch warrior against the "I just want to be happy" sentiment. "Tell me where in the Bible it says God wants us to be happy!" I have demanded on more than one occasion. God wants us to have His peace. God wants us to know His joy. But nowhere does it say God wants us to be happy. Gah!

I was wrong. Sort of.

God does want us to be happy. It's just that His definition of happiness and ours might be a smidge different. God wants us to be happy in Him. He wants us to find happiness in our relationship with Him. It's not about momentary happiness. That elusive feeling we pursue with relentless, reckless abandon.

God's desire for our happiness lies in Him and in Him alone. In the most intimate and loving and selfless relationship that one could ever dream or imagine. Entirely devoted. Entirely committed. An infinity x google amount of perfection. How crazy awesome is that?!

So, I stand corrected.

God does want us to be happy. Now, if I could only get out of my own way pursuing all these earthly desires to focus on the one true happiness ...

> "Because of You, I know the path of life, as I taste the fullness of joy in Your presence. At Your right side, I experience divine pleasures forevermore."
>
> **Psalm 16:11, TPT**

SELF AWARENESS

The deep water that reveals both our strengths and blind spots lead us to greater self-awareness, which is the foundation of personal growth. Too often, we drift through life on autopilot, outsourcing our decisions, our identities, and even our desires to the expectations of others. We read from a script someone else has written for us. But when we take ownership of our thoughts, actions, and direction, we step into a deeper, more authentic way of living—one that demands honesty, courage, and a willingness to truly see ourselves. And that, friends, is a giant leap forward toward living in freedom.

WHAT YOU WANT, BABY, I GOT IT

It's pumpkin spice latte and rush hour traffic and deep water moving faster than any car in Dallas/Ft. Worth.

"Which book would you like?" the store clerk asked.

"Surprise me," she replied.

"I don't have a book with that title."

Today's deep water is about personal responsibility. All too often, we give control to others. We might do this because we are being "cute," wanting to please others, being lazy, or simply being unwilling to take responsibility for our own choices.

If we trust others are sincere in their asking, "What do you like (or want, or need)?" this requires us to be honest in our reply.

> *"When Jesus saw him lying there and knew that he had already been there a long time, he said to him, "Do you want to be healed?"*
>
> **John 5:6, ESV**

Jesus Himself recognized our willingness to forgo taking responsibility for our well-being. Do we really want to be healed? Are we willing to give up what made us sick?

WHAT GIVES?

It's the boy's favorite chicory coffee in the pink floral mug and Florida-like summer afternoon rainstorms and 30 days until the little moves to Oxford ... Mississippi.

Life is about choices. You either choose by action or by inaction. Setting goals or aimlessly wandering.

Take time to determine your goals and take time to be realistic about what you are willing to sacrifice to attain those goals.

If your career is your goal, are you willing to sacrifice time with family, friends, and your health? If family is your goal, are you willing to sacrifice a higher level of success in business? If health, are you willing to sacrifice to eat clean or give up your leisure time?

Goals in life, success as you determine it, doesn't just happen. Achieving those goals requires honesty with yourself.

BROTHERLY LOVE

When you wake up at 4:00 a.m. you've gotta know serious deep water is coming your way.

Two brothers. One is a textbook rebel. Takes everything he can get from his father, runs away, and squanders it all. The other is the "good brother." He stays with the family and does the good work, the "correct" work. He's there through thick and thin. He is a good worker. The best worker. He honors his father with his work.

Seems pretty cut and dry, doesn't it? One son lives a life of rebellion, and the other lives the better life. But it's not quite so simple.

The rebellion is easy to grasp. But what if I told you the "good" son was just as messed up? Have you considered the good son lived a life of right and wrong? A life with only one path, a path of correctness? He was correct; his rebellious brother was not. He did things—did life— the "right" way, while his rebellious brother did not. The good son created as much division as his brother.

Neither brother lived a life of love. One chose rebellion, and the other chose ... religion. A spirit of right and wrong. Of superiority based on my behavior. My way or the highway.

Jesus lives in the middle of these brothers. Love lives there. Whether you rebel or demand adherence to some man-instituted standard, when you live out of anything other than love, you get it wrong.

> *"Beloved, if God so loved us, we also ought to love one another."*
>
> 1 John 4:11, ESV

POINT OF CONVERGENCE

It's a not-yet-healthy mocha in an unchosen mug and apple picking fun and missing the Mac time management.

What are you thinking? More precisely, what are you thinking about?

Where our mind is focused directs what we do. Just like body position and where we focus our eyes impacts a physical outcome, what we think about has a trajectory. Ask any athlete. Where he looks and how he points his body is going to determine where the ball goes.

Set your focus where you want to go. I'm not talking about all that positive mental attitude stuff. Good stuff, but not what the deep water is about today. If you want to be healthy, focus on the healthy. If you want to be happy, focus on the happy. If you want to be _____, focus on _____.

Focus, focus, focus. The lens of the camera. The lens of your life.

> "Since you have been raised to new life with Christ, set your sights on the realities of heaven, where Christ sits in the place of honor at God's right hand. Think about the things of heaven, not the things of earth."
>
> **Colossians 3:1-2, NLT**

THROW DOWN

It's an early start to the day and bright skies and the pink floral robe and reflective deep water.

Confidence breeds security. Knowing allows one to stand outside the argument. Have you ever noticed that Jesus never argued? Think about it. He knew the truth, all truth, and never once felt compelled to argue. It's a pretty amazing thing to witness someone so confident in who they are, the absolute truth of things, that there is no need to argue.

Arguing is a straightforward look into someone's confidence. It illuminates who they are and where they stand with themselves (and others).

> "It was as if they realized, as I did not, that my attitude and my desire of argument ... implied a fundamental and utter lack of faith, and a dependence on my own lights, and attachment to my own opinion."
>
> **Thomas Merton,** *The Seven Story Mountain*

What do you know? How do you stand in that truth?

HE SAID WHAT?!

The family dinner and Cabernet are done and the little is as snug as a bug and the deep water is all about hearing voices.

My first coach. His voice. All that he has inspired in me (and so very many) was instantly rekindled at the sound of his voice. Youthful memories of swimming in the slow lane and this coach seeing me—really seeing the promise in me, turned my life's page and made me a swimmer. That page-turner changed me. Forever.

I was interviewing for a new job this week. One of the questions asked where I positioned myself on an athletic team. "I'm the anchor," I replied so quickly everyone in the room was caught off guard. I know where I'm best, where I've been the best because this man spoke truth and potential into my life. I know who I am, in no small part, because of his voice.

God's voice speaks life and truth and potential, just like my beloved coach, but for each of us. In and out of the pool. Whose voice do you listen to? What does it say?

GIMME! GIMME! GIMME!

It's a keto coffee in the Texas mug and dogs begging for attention to start the day and pivotal deep water.

Would you ask a butcher for a donut? How about asking a dentist to repair your roof? Pretty silly, huh? Still, we ask the wrong people to be a source for providing what we need every single day.

It takes insight and maturity to recognize what we need. It takes time and attention to recognize what we are asking of others and whether or not they are truly capable of giving that which we ask. It doesn't mean the other person isn't good or kind or even absolutely the best ever. But it does mean not every person can fill your needs exactly as you need them filled.

Be self-aware when asking. Be other-aware, too. Our deepest requests can only be filled when we ask for what others are equipped to give. Oftentimes, it's a request only God Himself can fill.

YOU HAVE MADE FOR YOURSELF GODS

It's coffee and heavy cream in the pretty Poland mug and another day for the fun rain boots and receiving deep water.

When opportunity presents itself, do you run to it, run from it, or pray about it? Do you push forward, soaking up everything, exhausted from soaking up everything, or do you step back and prayerfully evaluate?

So often, we say yes to opportunity because it's there. Because being asked feels good. Working/winning/putting our best before our idols feels good. It fills us. Until it doesn't.

Not everything in front of you is for you. It may be yours for the taking, but it isn't necessarily for the betterment of who God created you to be. Where are your treasures? How do you spend your time? Is it all for the glory of God or the glory of you?

NOT MY RESPONSIBILITY

It's an almond milk keto-friendly latte in a paper cup and Midwest humidity and the weekend!

How often do we wholeheartedly jump into something on the word of another? Business. Healthy living. Politics. "But so-and-so is someone I trust." Awesome.

Until it isn't.

Today's deep water is all about taking personal responsibility for what we do with what we hear, even from reliable sources, especially from reliable sources. Ultimately, it's about maturity and personal responsibility. It's far easier to make someone else responsible for what we think and do than to own our thoughts and actions. In a fast-paced world, it's easier to grab-and-go than it is to stop and consider. Responsibility takes time.

> *"We demolish arguments and every pretension that sets itself up against the knowledge of God, and we take captive every thought to make it obedient to Christ."*
>
> **2 Corinthians 10:5, NIV**

ROSE-COLORED GLASSES

It's a London Fog tea in the Texas mug and weekday sleepover fun and a great deep water truth bomb.

The lens we use to see the "other side" is seldom the same lens we use to examine our side. We inherently filter through rose-colored glasses, seeing only the highlights and happiness of "over there." It is far easier to be lazily critical of my own grass while simultaneously being overly enthusiastic about the ease with which the other side is made greener.

Much like a house prepped for sale suddenly becoming so much more lovely, our efforts on our own behalf—personally, relationally—have a tangible impact. When we water the life within our own four walls, that life will become so much more lovely. Our weeds will be diminished, and our grass will be a deeper, more vibrant green. Watering your own grass. Now, there's a novel concept.

I CAN'T HEAR YOU

It's an almond milk latte in the "because adulting is hard" mug and new summer pajamas and a boisterous start to the day.

A pickup truck roared down the street. It interrupted my quiet time. Ugh! Why always this need to make a statement? A loud statement? Has anyone ever heard about walking softly and carrying a big stick?

It seems more people go through the day with an unnecessarily loud bark. There is such a profound need to be loud. It's more than the need to be heard. It is an angry need to be heard over everyone else. To know that you cannot be ignored.

Oh, the deep water.

As we become more and more disconnected (thank you, technology), we become louder and louder. We yearn to be heard. We crave the connection of having someone really listen. Absent that connection, we will grow more forceful in making ourselves heard and known. Ultimately, we will strong-arm our way into being heard.

> *"Know this, my beloved brothers: let every person be quick to hear, slow to speak, slow to anger."*
>
> **James 1:19, ESV**

PHILOSOPHY 101

It's espresso and heavy cream in the pretty pink mug and woot—cold weather! ... and the little's "if you're not puking, you're not running hard enough" cross country conference meet.

It's a thoughtful beginning to the day. Descartes at 7:00 is weighty, but there you have it. "I think therefore I am" is fairly well known. But the deep water completes the phrase.

"I doubt, therefore I think. I think, therefore, I am."

A good thinker, a thorough thinker, always welcomes doubt. Doubting allows for revelation, a necessary step in wisdom.

Whatever you're thinking, make sure you check yourself. Just because you're thinking it doesn't make it so.

> "Examine yourselves to see whether you are in the faith. Test yourselves. Or do you not realize this about yourselves, that Jesus Christ is in you?—unless indeed you fail to meet the test!"
>
> **2 Corinthians 13:5, ESV**

LIKE A PAIR OF WELL-WORN SHOES

It's a bottle of Powerade Zero® and another 12 ounces of water and wishing I'd put on a heavier sweater and best friend deep water.

Don't you just love being comfortable? Comfortable feels soooo good. "Leave me alone, let me be. I'm gonna just settle in here, all comfy cosy."

Unless you're just settling.

The deep water calls out comfortable. It's easy to find others who will let us stay where we are, as we are. It's comforting when others let us be comfortable. Not much happens in comfortable land.

How about we find people who want more out of life than being comfortable? How about we seek those who aren't content to let themselves, or us, settle?

Cheers to uncomfortable.

THE GREEN, GREEN GRASS OF HOME

It's an LMNT citrus water in the pink Stanley and autumn breezes and wearing jeans for the first time this season happiness.

Smack your mama truth bomb incoming.

The grass is NOT greener.

Water the grass where you are first. Give that grass all the chances to grow, and you along with it. Don't walk through today with one foot out the door into tomorrow. It's only when you are fully invested in today, the grass of where you are now, that you even have a chance to see what God intends for you. Looking to that other grass, the grass that looks greener, deprives you of all the blessings and goodness and opportunities and, dare I say, fun of today.

Grow where you're planted.

A DOG WITH A BONE

It's the summer robe covered in dragonflies and an almond milk latte in a mug covered in bears and the deep water is courtesy of the Catahoula—a morning full of animals!

The crazy Cajun (a.k.a. Doug, the dog) has decided a hole needs to be dug. He has found THE place and will not be deterred. We fill it in. We cover it with new sod. We sprinkle cayenne pepper over it. Nonetheless, it is his location for his hole, and he is going to accomplish his work. Woe to us who interfere.

And there it is. This dog is passionate about his work. He won't let any of us crazy humans get in his way. Daily, he endeavors to do the work to which he feels called.

So, how do you and I compare in pursuing our callings? You know, the work to which God has called us? How often do we let "crazy humans" get in our way? Divert our efforts? Sideline us? How often do we let the crazy human we call me, myself, and I get in our way?

And what if today's calling isn't work as we commonly define it? What if today's work is to increase your relationship with the Heavenly Father? Yet another layer to today's deep water ...

Our greatest calling is to be in intimate relationship with God. It is the first and greatest commandment. Love your God with all your heart, all your soul, and all your mind. Do we accomplish this commandment of loving as passionately as Doug pursues digging his hole?

MIRROR, MIRROR ON THE WALL

It's a second latte at the DC house and a still injured foot and well and...

Have you ever been in a season of discernment? Modern life doesn't seem to afford us time to discern. As a result, when we find ourselves in seasons of discernment, things can often seem off-balance, out of whack, upside down, and inside out. And that is where God's deep water for today resides.

God never intended for us to live smooth, easy lives absent introspection. One of the easiest ways Satan can come between us and God is to keep us from focusing on God. By keeping us exponentially "busy," Satan keeps us from taking the time to look at ourselves and the choices we are making in life and recalibrate. He keeps our focus selfish and self-centered—on all of the things that we "have" to do and all of the things that we "should" do. It completely distracts us from the one thing we are obligated to do, which is to increase our relationship with Christ Himself and, as an extension of that, others.

Taking the time to discern who we are, how we are living our lives, and most importantly, how we walk with God seems out of step with culture today. Taking the time to discern is an opportunity to set relationships and priorities right. Contrary to popular belief, setting aside time to discern in our own personal lives is not selfish. It is quite the contrary, allowing us to be "self-less" (less of self) in focusing on God and others.

> *"He must become greater and greater, and I must become less and less."*
>
> **John 3:30, NLT**

SELF TALK

It's the cold remnants of an almond milk latte in the pretty Poland mug and goin' to see my Mama prep and soon-to-be-spoken truth.

What are you thinking? Better yet, what do you think about what you are thinking?

Kinda confusing. Or is it? I think there are some pretty good reasons the Bible tells us to take every thought captive and hold it up to the scrutiny of the Word, to the scrutiny of Jesus.

If I tell myself I have failed, I limit myself. Actually, I do more than limit myself. I become the very thing I speak. I become a failure.

Now, that isn't at all true, but what I say to myself has consequences. I can direct my steps with what I say. I can learn from the choices I have made, both positive and negative, successful and unsuccessful, or I can pigeonhole myself by carrying the weight of what hasn't gone my way.

What you do is not who you are. What you tell yourself matters.

> "Guard your heart above all else, for it determines the course of your life."
>
> **Proverbs 4:23, NLT**

WHITE WASHED TOMBS

It's the now daily pumpkin cinnamon roll coffee in the pretty Poland mug and fingers-crossed waiting and sick days.

It is the one addiction we don't condemn. It is the one addiction we actually applaud. It is, despite the apparent accolades, still an addiction.

They are busy, busy, busy. Working day and night. Work, work, work. Go, go, go. Text messages. iPads. Laptops. Desktops. A cell phone in each hand. Their clients need them. Their bosses need them. They are needed. Important. Essential. 24/7. They never stop.

Workaholics live The Life. They travel to all the places. Live in the pretty houses. Eat at the fancy restaurants. Have all the biggest and best, latest and greatest. They aren't keeping up with the Joneses; they are the Joneses. And they are missing the mark.

For all their effort, workaholics are the last people you'd call lazy. They are the epitome of just the opposite. And yet ... If you keep busy enough, you won't have to do your work. You won't have the time or the bandwidth to see yourself. You can avoid the mirror. You can run from personal demons and choices and consequences. You can busy yourself right into the laziness of an unexamined life.

This, you see, is what busy-ness does to us. It prevents us from remaining focused on the most important work that we need to do.

SING, SING A SONG

It's one last latte and the bittersweet of wrapping up the trip of a lifetime and the sweetest deep water ever.

This week's deep water is all about, well, the deep water.

Trade winds and white caps quickly overrun morning calm seas in Maui. The swimmer in me, however, could not, would not be dissuaded by the seemingly agitated water. I left the Mac closer to shore and made my way out to deeper water. And then into deeper water still. And then it happened …

Despite being alone and small-ish white caps, I turned on my back and floated. Water feels like home to me. More like home than anywhere else. As I surrendered to the motion of the sea, I heard it. Heard them.

Humpback whales winter 100-200 yards offshore here. And if you relax into the sea and listen, you can hear them calling to one another. No microphone. No amplification. I floated, and I listened, and I heard them … again and again.

I wonder how many times we stay close to the things and people we know instead of venturing out alone. I wonder how many times the white caps of life deter us from being still and listening.

Find the space, like Jesus did, to be alone and listen to God. He may just serenade you with whale songs.

"Be still, and know that I am God!"

Psalm 46:10a, NLT

ME, MYSELF, AND I

It's a healthy pumpkin spice latte in the new and most beloved pumpkin mug and autumn virus yuck and church in bed.

When did it happen? When did you become so comfortable with giving up when things got hard? There was a season, maybe even many seasons, where you persisted despite innumerable challenges. So, I'm wondering when giving up became part of you.

For me, it's been a gradual and sometimes slippery slope. Understanding and growing into a healthy relationship with perfectionism, there were legitimate times when giving up was the wise thing to do. The next thing you know, giving up and giving in became the easy thing to do, and then it became the typical thing to do.

Overachieving has, not in everything but enough things, segued into letting it all go. In my quiet moments, I speculate if this is what a midlife crisis is all about. Is this why people recalibrate when they hit their 50s?

For me this isn't about a sexy new car or something to make me feel like I'm 20 again. For me, it's about being responsible for my health and well-being. I've spent the better part of the last 30 years caring for others and achieving athletic goals for myself, but not really taking care of myself. I am realizing that taking care of myself has to be a priority. Not to the neglect of my faith or my husband or my family and friends, but so that I can be strong in those things.

So many times, religion tells us that we have to put others first and that any effort towards self is misguided at best. Pretty compelling, but a total lie.

> *"Love others as you love yourself."*
> Leviticus 19:18

As you love yourself. Fill your cup to overflowing so you have the resources to fill others.

ATTENTION, K-MART SHOPPERS

It's a healthy peppermint mocha in the naughty or nice mug and the most wonderful time of the year and laying the groundwork for prayerful efforts.

Hey! Hey, you!

I NEED YOUR ATTENTION!

Not really. But there are and always will be people demanding your attention. In business, it looks like an inbox. In life, it looks like an overfilled calendar with so, so much to do and not enough hours in the day.

Whoever and whatever is demanding that your time fit their agenda, watch out. Keep a strong hold on your time and your goals. Just because it is delivered in a polite manner doesn't mean it's for you.

> *"Pay careful attention to your own work, for then you will get the satisfaction of a job well done, and won't need to compare yourself to anyone else. For we are each responsible for our own conduct."*
>
> **Galatians 6:4-5, NLT**

OPEN MOUTHS GET FED

It's a nutty Irishman in a paper cup and another town another coffee shop solo adventures and we're back in the south familiarity.

It's a lie, you know? The notion that if someone knows you well enough, really and truly loves you enough, and cares enough, they will "just know" what you need and want. Complete bunk.

> *"A closed mouth doesn't get fed."*
> Kevin Daniels

Deep water bomb.

Girlfriend! Someone's ability (or inability) to read your mind, anticipate your needs and wants, satisfy the deepest desires of your hidden self ... that's on you. Gah! Stop it!

But it's true. A closed mouth doesn't get fed. If you aren't getting what you need or want out of a relationship, speak up. Be bold. Be brave. Be unwavering in your commitment to being honest with yourself and others. God included.

Another familiar variant of the quote:

> *"You do not have because you do not ask."*
> James 4:2b, ESV

Being seen and not heard is not problem-solving. It isn't taking one for the team. It isn't being selfless. It isn't preferring others over self. Think about it for a minute (or ten). Before you can love your neighbor as yourself, you must first know and love yourself. You must know who and what and how God fashioned you and your callings and desires. Knowing yourself requires effort. And honesty. And grace. And in learning all about you, you may just acquire skills that will facilitate you being able to know and love others well.

It's a give-and-take. Know yourself. Share what you know. Ask for what you need. All those steps open the door for others to be known. Not mind reading. Asking. Learning. Loving.

PERFORMANCE

Living a performance-based life centers around the idea that our worth and success are determined by what we do. But what if our value and identity are not about the doing at all? What if it is found in exploring the truth that being—who we are in Christ—holds far more value than our ability to perform or achieve? As a lifelong performance addict, I can tell you that discovering this key unlocks the door to levels of freedom I never even imagined were possible!

NOT BY WORKS

It's a nutty Irishman latte in a pink paper cup and the first day of high school for our freshman and descaling so I can have the coffee.

I'm a proficient do-er. Ask any of my friends, mentors, anybody really. I can "do" with the best of them. And I work really hard at not being broken. I do healing and working to be healed every single day. Do. Do. Do. Oh my goodness, I need some more be-ing help for sure!

I don't like the brokenness. I so want to be whole. Entirely whole, in Christ. Can I please just work myself into wholeness?!?!

And there's the deep water. Front and center.

It is in our brokenness Christ's light shines.

> "But He said to me, 'My grace is sufficient for you, for my power is made perfect in weakness.' Therefore, I will boast all the more gladly about my weaknesses so that Christ's power may rest on me."
>
> **2 Corinthians 12:9, NIV**

WHAT CAN I DO?

It's an almond milk latte in the Lake City mug and walking with Doug the dog and deep water in progress.

My spiritual director and I have been working on something for a while now. It began with one of our first meetings, and I remember her words of wisdom changed my perspective. "Maybe it's not what God wants you to do, Jackie, but who He wants you to be." Ummm …

Are you a performer? Is your success in the world, in the eyes of loved ones, in your eyes, based on what and how well you do? If only you could "do it the right way." "If you'd just tell me what you want. What can I do?!"

It's been a process. It is a process. But I believe my friend and mentor had it correct. It's not about the do-ing. It's about the be-ing. Once you get that right, the rest will come from the overflow, and it will be amazing.

I am learning to put intimacy above activity, abiding before serving, and authentic life before a projected image.

> *"If you abide (that's a being word) in My Word, you are truly My disciples, and you will know the truth, and the truth will set you free."*
>
> **John 8:32, ESV (parenthesis added)**

Free indeed, friends. Free indeed.

FIRST PLACE

It's a Mac-made coffee in the pretty Poland mug and cosy clothes amidst status quo Ohio winter weather and so so much deep water the cup has become an aquifer.

January. New year. New goals. New plans. New, well, whatever you want. Because it's January. Time to set all those new things in motion. Time to set (and reset) your priorities.

But ... not so fast, dear ones. Deep water oxymoronic life-altering shift in-coming.

You cannot have more than one priority.

The word priority, by its very definition, means first. It is a singular directive placing one thing above the others. Kinda like first place is first place, but second place is first loser mentality.

The word priority originated from the Latin word "prior," meaning first. At some point in the 20th century, priority was demoted to its current plural form—priorities.

Demoted. Reduced. Diluted.

You see, when we have more than one master, we have none. When we have more than one priority, we actually have none. Multitasking isn't often effective as it distracts and diverts. It doesn't allow for A priority.

When bolstered by a singular directive, A priority, everything else in life, in business, and in all endeavors falls into place. When you know your WHY, you are able to make better choices for all else.

Today, I encourage you to take time and reflect on your priority. The one thing that counts above all else. I can almost certainly guarantee you that doing so will lead to the life you dream of (or something like it).

> *"Rather, seek first His kingdom and His righteousness, and all these things will be given to you as well."*
>
> **Matthew 6:33, NIV (emphasis added)**

KINTSUGI

It's the healthy mocha in the pretty Poland mug and a day of joyful anticipation and the sun peeking through the clouds.

Lent. The perfect season to remind us of imperfect observation. Slips. Stumbles. Epic falls. Failing to observe Lent well.

I am reminded it has never been about performing. It is not about perfection. Lent is an opportunity to acknowledge a complete lack on our part.

In Japanese tradition, the silver or gold-filled cracks in a vessel render it more valuable. It is in the mending of the brokenness that strength and value are to be found. And lauded. It is in the brokenness we find Jesus.

> *"And we know that God causes everything to work together for the good of those who love God and are called according to His purpose for them."*
>
> **Romans 8:28, NLT**

JUDGEY MCJUDGEPANTS

It's the healthy latte in the pretty pink floral mug and another morning with the resurrected winter robe and 0-dark-thirty wake-up calls from a scamp of a puppy.

I have a friend. (Yeah, I know. It's true.) And she gave me some very sound advice recently. She challenged me, truth be told. You see, I was being a bit judgmental. More than a bit. And the person I was judging was none other than ... me.

Goals. Plans to execute to reach the goals. Accountability along the way. And I kept giving myself failing or almost failing grades. I saw all the progress that needed to be made and little, if any, of the work I had already done. Work I had done well. Alas, it mattered not to me, myself, and I. I hadn't completed the tasks. I had not reached the goal. And, thus, I was ... failing.

Stop the madness! Now, my dearest of friends was not harsh. She uttered no words of criticism or condemnation. She gently asked me to consider the progress I had made. To give myself the deserved marks for what I had already completed.

Ladies and gentlemen. The truth of today's deep water is this: perfection is not the goal. Completion is a long-off target with lots of itsy-bitsy steps along the way. Each step is vital. Each step gets its own grade. Doesn't mean every little achievement deserves a trophy, but it does deserve celebration.

Today, I'm smiling at crawling before I walk.

DO YOUR JOB

It's a gingerbread latte in the pumpkin mug and finding a home in the aftermath of boxes and the autumn stack of reading delivered courtesy of Amazon.

> *"Do your job."*
> Bill Belichick

I like to have something to listen to while cleaning, unpacking, and chasing the puppy. Series. Mini-series. Documentaries. This week's choice: "Becoming the G.O.A.T.: The Tom Brady Story."

The deep water is both restrictive and empowering at the same time. Do. Your. Job. Be entirely focused on what you need to do. Your job. Give your best and learn and grow and better yourself. So you can do your job.

I know, I know. I opened this section by talking about being and not doing. I meant FOCUSING on being BEFORE doing. I mean doing FROM being. Okay? Now that that's settled, we can get back to talking about the job we are called to do.

It is only when we have the clarity of doing our singular job and doing it well that others can do their job. A team doesn't require a Jack of All Trades. A successful team requires each individual to do their job to the best of their ability.

It's like that in life as well. A company requires different people to do different jobs. All are essential to the running of the company. A sports team requires the same. A sewing guild. An orchestra. A family. A marriage.

You can and should not be all things to all people. You cannot "have it all." And I beg the question, "Should you?"

The deep water is a lifter of position and person today. Do your job.

Allow others to do theirs. Do your job well. An arm never longed to be a foot. Jesus never longed to be anything but himself. He had a job to do.

Keep up the work. Good work. Do your job. Do it well. See your job in the light of the bigger picture.

> *"There is one body, but it has many parts ... if one part suffers, every part suffers with it. If one part is honored, every part shares in its joy. You are the body of Christ. Each one of you is a part of it."*
>
> **1 Corinthians 12:12-27, NIV**

NEEDY NELLY

It's a twig tea in the bear paw mug and bracing for winter and restful afternoons after much exploring.

I have always had to be okay—even when I wasn't. Healthy or sick. Stability or upheaval. Perception or reality.

I. Must. Always. Be. Okay.

Okay means I won't be a problem. I will not disrupt or upset. I will require nothing from no one. I am not, nor will I ever, be needy. Needy is bad. Needy is a problem.

Deep water alert! God loves us in our neediness. Needing is an opportunity to love and be loved.

I'm not sure when I'll grow into being comfortable in my needs, but today is a moment of hopeful clarity.

God meets you. Meets your needs.

> *"And my God will fully supply all your needs out of the riches of His glory in Christ Jesus."*
> **Philippians 4:19, NCB**

NOT MY CUP OF TEA

It's a cup of Twig Tea in the Jane mug and morning devotions with the Mac and a back-in-the-saddle kind of day.

Today's deep water is, well, dang! I don't want to think it, let alone believe it's true kind of reality.

> Even when we try our best, we may not hit the mark for someone else.
>
> Keep on doing your best, and … God's got the rest.

NEVER ENOUGH

Jump off the cliff-deep water. No prelude.

If everything is A THING, then we are creating a culture of stressed-out, overthinking achievers or a culture of open rebellion in the face of never being secure or sufficient.

> *"And which of you by being anxious can add a single hour to his span of life?"*
>
> **Matthew 6:27, ESV**

SCRUPULOSITY AT ITS FINEST

It's a crazy early morning—a latte and a mug of drinking chocolate—and it's not even 7:00. And winter is upon us. Oh and there's the deep water.

I've spent the better part of 49 years trying to do it right. Part of the personal mandate to make the right choice and behave in the right manner stems from self-protection, but part of it stems from misguided faith practices. The sense that we can do enough, be enough, and earn God's approval is just wrong. It leads to shiny houses and smiles on Sunday and "I'm too blessed to be stressed" dishonesty.

A lot of us understand we can't earn our way to salvation but still hold on to the notion we must live rightly to gain God's approval and acceptance. We are hamsters on a wheel, trying our darnedest, and completely miss the mark.

What if, for today, we give our best because it's our best, not seeking a reward but trusting the gift?

> *"They receive God's approval freely by an act of His kindness..."*
>
> **Romans 3:24a, GW**

EMBRACE THE MESS

It's almond milk creamer and coffee in a worn Miami mug and morning quiet and borrowed deep water.

I have this friend. No, seriously. She is 30 years younger than I. It's amazing to be in a relationship with her. One of the blessings is how freely she shares her experience and wisdom. I love how learning isn't one way.

I might be a bit of a perfectionist. (I'm working on that.) And this dear friend shared what may be one of the most freeing phrases I've encountered. I'm going to chew on it for a while. Try it on. God's smiling—I just know it.

"Sloppy success vs. perfect failure"

Enjoy your sloppiness.

HEARTFELT DISCIPLINE

It's an Italian spritz and sunset by the sea and days of exploring.

My spiritual mentor reminds me, in the most compelling of manners, that discipline is a good thing when done from a heart perspective toward God and others. Too often, I find myself trying to be disciplined from a head perspective, earning my way into good-enough-ness.

Where do you base your discipline?

MAKE ME PROUD

It's the last latte in the very worn Miami mug and sun and birds singing and deep water on top of personal struggle.

He'd just completed a really "big" job. It was done well by society's standards. Done well by the church's standards. Many were blessed as a result of his job, done well.

"God, are you proud of me now?" he asked.

"Sweetheart," his wife replied, "God was proud of you before you even woke up this morning."

It is not about your performance.

> *"He happily rejoices over you, renews you with His love, and celebrates over you with shouts of joy."*
>
> **Zephaniah 3:17b, GW**

ENOUGH, ALRIGHT ALREADY

Well it's too late for coffee but a glass of red is a nice alternative. The Mac is stranded in Atlanta the big is finishing up exams in Montana the middle is "studying" for IB exams and the little is taking out his aggression on the pitchback.

The deep water swallows me whole sometimes, kinda like Jonah. I'm doing my thing, thinking I'm all good with God, and then, out of nowhere, I find myself swimming in the darkest of dark depths.

I just returned from serving on a retreat. The bestie and I were discussing and debriefing, and I asked, a heartfelt, be-my-mentor ask, "Was there anything I could have done better?" I am serving God and these daughters of the King. It was sincere. And my mentor saw right through it and me.

Deep water through-ness.

When we move from obedience to performance, we miss the mark. God asks for our obedience, not our perfection. He wants excellence, but that notwithstanding, He wants our obedience.

"Follow me." "Love God with all your heart, mind …" My friend pointed out that my obedience to the calling was enough. In my obedience, I was enough. I am enough.

LEAVE THEM WONDERING

It's a long-ago almond milk latte in the pretty Poland mug and early spring mornings spent 'round the fireplace and winter scarves and sweaters when you refuse to wear the winter coat any longer.

It's alright, you know? To say no and just leave it there. To say no thank you and not offer an explanation. It is 100% acceptable.

Well ... But ...

To those who take your "no" personally? Let them.

To those who insist on an explanation? Smile. Say nothing more. Walk away. It'll leave them wondering.

You see. Here's the thing. When we insist on explaining, we aren't comfortable with our "no." When others insist on an explanation, they aren't comfortable with our "no." Nowhere, ever, under the guise of good manners or etiquette is anyone obligated to explain their "no." It isn't polite. It isn't anything. It's just a bad habit continued by good people lacking healthy boundaries.

"Wow, Jackie! A bit strong in the deep water today, aren't we?"

I used to be top-of-the-class in making sure my "no" felt acceptable to me and, perhaps more so, to the recipient. The whole "make everyone happy with me" scenario. Here's the thing. I always felt like a beggar, pleading for release from whatever negative consequences I envisioned by saying no. I imagined it. Or I didn't. Either way, unless it is your spouse or an opportunity to train a child, you do not need to explain yourself.

I'm on my soapbox this morning. No, nothing happened. I am just watching all the songbirds and woodpeckers do their thing. They never explain. It's beautiful. Doing what they were created to do without hesitation or reservation or apology.

I want to be like the birds.

GOAL-SETTER, GO-GETTER

It's a Mac-made beverage in the Hochatown mug and fall fireplace cosyness and learning lessons each and every day.

The deep water is all about rewriting and rewiring these days. Completely upending standard operating procedures.

Goals are good, right?

Yes. And no.

The great thing about goals is that they are a motivating target. The not-so-great thing about goals is that they are an end in and of themselves. Once you've reached your goal, you're done. Finished. Complevit. So, what's an alternative?

Have you considered that agreeing to "being" is a more consistent and continuous alternative? Be what your goal requires you to be. Be a marathoner. Be a cook. Be a reader. Be a _____. Within the "be-ing" are myriad opportunities for success. Without an end. Without the need to rewrite or reconfigure your next success.

Be-ing. Ultimately the more consistent and continuous method than goal setting. Being changes you as a person. Not just for a moment, but forever. We are, after all, made in His image, are we not?

"I AM WHO I AM."

Exodus 3:14, NASB

ALL THAT YOU ARE

It's a healthy mocha in the Lake City mug and new colors and 5:00 AM puppy mornings.

Whoa, Nelly. This morning's deep water came out of nowhere and—no joke—changed everything. One of the A-team enlightened me. Shared a grace-filled lens that, once realized, cannot be put away.

In discussing our fears, I shared that I was afraid of not being all God created me to be. Falling short. All that performance stuff (again) front and center. Deep water washed all over it, thanks to her.

Would you think less of a 3-year-old for being 3? An 18-year-old for being 18? What if God is perfectly, wonderfully happy with who you are and how He loves you now? And if you are enough for Him as you are, AND He loves you enough to watch you continue to grow? To become?

You, dear one, are enough of who you were created to be right now. You will be more tomorrow. And the days and months and years after. It's a process.

God loves you today.

"... first the blade, then the ear, then the full grain in the ear."
Mark 4:28b, ESV

ADVERSITY

Adversity usually hits when we least expect it, shaking us to our core and forcing us to reckon with our limits. Yet, through these struggles, we often find unexpected grace and strength—lessons that, when we yield to them, shape us into something more resilient and deeper than before. The challenges we face, while painful, can become the very catalysts that transform us, guiding us toward growth and peace.

THE FLIP SIDE

It's a Biggby cold brew in the largest cup they have and sunshine to melt the snow and signing day! Woohoo!

Today's deep water came at me fast and hard. As in, "Sit down, shut up, and pay some serious attention to me right now!" fast and hard.

What if your biggest struggle turns into your biggest grace? What if that thing in your marriage that you just can't work out turns into the very thing you need most from your marriage? What if the subject you just can't master leads you to the class in which you excel? What if the sport you were forced to quit due to injury opens the door to the sport you'll enjoy for a lifetime?

WHAT IF?

It's an iced coffee in the new iced coffee tumbler and tree felling chain saws to serenade and cool tile floors in the summer.

So often we fight against what we think we know want and need only to find out its absence is THE grace that leads to our peace our joy and our success.

Don't close the door when not perfect, not great, or not good seemingly "ruins" your day. Who knows? It just may be the best thing to ever happen in your tomorrow.

> *"We can rejoice, too, when we run into problems and trials, for we know they help us develop endurance. And endurance develops strength of character, and character strengthens our confident hope of salvation. And this hope will not lead to disappointment ..."*
>
> **Romans 5:3-5, NLT**

SEMPER GUMBY

The sun is thinking about setting. It's Chimney Rock Cabernet to drink. The Williams-Sonoma apron reminds me dinner is usually more than salami and manchego.

Today's deep water is all about silly putty. Being silly putty. It is a lesson for those moments when everything is changing. Things are good, but in such a state of flux that you don't know if you're coming or going. When that happens, it's best to remember how resilient silly putty is. You can mush it, mash it, push and pull it. You can twist it back on itself in some pretty unimaginable ways. And yet. It remains intact. It is flexible in the truest sense of the word, but strong, reliable. Even if it breaks, you can put it back together, and it will be just as strong as it ever was.

God uses the challenges of the world to remind us we are as flexible and resilient as silly putty.

> *"I know how to be brought low, and I know how to abound. In any and every circumstance, I have learned the secret of facing plenty and hunger, abundance and need. I can do all things through Him who strengthens me."*
>
> **Philippians 4:12-13, ESV**

RISE ABOVE

The sun is hidden above rain clouds it's Love tea in the cup and the winter robe is back in the closet replaced by the clothes of the day.

Today's Collect comes from the Book of Common Prayer, and it hits home (once again).

> *"... Preserve us that we may not ... be overcome by adversity."*

The Bible promises us we will have tribulations, trials, and troubles in this life. Even when we recognize this truth, there are days when those burdens come hard and fast and in droves. It is not only comforting but powerful to pray that we not be overcome by those challenges which could so easily dissuade us from walking upright in His peace and joy.

Today, rather than focusing on not "letting the buggers get me down," I am focusing on the strength and provision of God to keep me from being overcome by adversity. Surely, God can do much more than keep me from being kept down; He can strengthen me to rise above.

> *"Great peace have those who love Your law; nothing can make them stumble."*
>
> **Psalm 119:165, ESV**

MOGULS

It's a healthy pumpkin spice latte in the beloved pumpkin mug and the first day of autumn celebration and three hours in the MRI tube just to prove I still have MS.

God is concerned more about our character than our comfort level.

Buckle up, friends. We're in for a bumpy ride.

That phrase always seems a bit daunting. Being told to buckle up and prepare for a bumpy ride. And with good reason. We should be braced against the bumps. It's a wise and healthy safety measure. But let's get incredibly technical for a minute, shall we?

What is a bump in the road? Well, it means that 1) you've been on a smooth ride, 2) you're going up a hill, or 3) you're coming down a hill. Technically, a bump is just a really, really, really small hill in your road. And lots of really small hills in the midst of your smooth path can feel uncomfortable.

We don't like discomfort. Most of us prefer the smooth, newly paved road. Some of us will even take the nicely worn path. No major bumps. No major divots. No hills or valleys.

This morning's deep water reminds me that growth doesn't happen without resistance. Bumps in the road teach us something. Lots of bumps = lots of lessons. And there is grace in the learning. It teaches us to be gentle with ourselves. To be gentle with others. To love as Christ loved, especially when things are hard. That is when we most need to love and be loved—when we are in the middle of the bumpy road.

This morning, as I lay in that MRI tube and the cacophony of sound bumps runs over me again and again and again, I'm going to focus on all the smooth roads I've walked. I'm going to focus on the graces in my life. I'm going to tune out the almost painful noise, and instead, I am going to ask God to show me where the lessons are and where the love resides.

"Therefore, the Lord waits to be gracious to you ..."

Isaiah 30:18, ESV

HOW YOU DOIN'?

The sun has finally brought warmth to North Texas. It's been a sweet tea kind of day. The deep water came early but I've been standing in it trying to grasp the message.

Three hours into a 3 1/2 hour MRI, I heard the words, "Everything's not fine, and I'm not okay ..." and I thought, "Wow. Do I know that?! I really know that." Being in an MRI for over 3 hours really doesn't allow anyone to hide from what's not fine and how not okay they really are. MS just stinks. Period.

But. And it is the ultimate BUT ... it's nice to know that even in the midst of horrendous "I'm not fine" moments, God is with us. Individually. Personally. And He can take the tough stuff. He's got it. He's got you. He's got me. If you saw me, you really wouldn't know I have MS. And for that, I'm grateful beyond words. But I do deal with it—every single moment of every single day.

Everything is not fine. I'm not okay. And you know what? God is there with me, and that is more than enough.

> *"The Lord Himself goes before you and will be with you; He will never leave you nor forsake you. Do not be afraid; do not be discouraged."*
>
> **Deuteronomy 31:8, NIV**

NO PAIN, NO GAIN

A beautiful salmon sky to start the day. It's vanilla almond milk creamer in the cup. No time for sitting in a comfy robe—there are things to do places to go and people to see.

Today's deep water lies at the intersection of athletic (and some would say life) success and the Resurrection. Let's dive ...

"No pain, no gain." We all know it. Athletes know it well. Our success-driven culture espouses it. Clothing companies trademark it. It is what we do. During my walk this morning, it was pressed upon me that perhaps we paint too broadly with this motto. It doesn't hold water for Christians.

It's true that the world brings struggle. Suffering. But we are not meant to seek it out. We are not meant to look for pain as the source of our gain. Quite the contrary. In the Resurrection, Jesus assumed all the pain we will experience. He experienced our pain during His life, and He assumed our sin upon the cross. He gave us a way out of the pain. A direct line to the Father. "It is finished." Jesus completed the work. All the work. And that work allows us to rest and have peace in God. We don't need to push through pain as a means for gain. We can take the pain and give it to God. The strength we gain in giving our pain and suffering to God far exceeds anything we can build for ourselves by pushing through on our own.

> *"That according to the riches of His glory, He may grant you to be strengthened with power through His Spirit in your inner being."*
>
> **Ephesians 3:16, ESV**

CLEAN UP ON AISLE 9

It's coffee with almond creamer in the "OH HAPPY DAY" mug and yet another day too hot for a morning robe and shocking deep water.

She is our princess. Our sweet little Sheltie. She wouldn't harm the hair on a flea.

He is our crazy cajun. He's ripped, literally. A fit, sporting dog who just wants to play with anything and everything he sees. Unfortunately for his puppy self, he's terribly naughty in his enthusiasm. Not mean-spirited, but playful beyond boundaries.

Imagine my shock when the crazy cajun walked over to our sweet princess, lifted his leg, and … all over her. What the heck?!?!

In the midst of this unexpected chaos, the deep water.

How many times are we living our lives, minding our own business, not harming the hair on a flea, and "wham" Satan lifts his leg and … ? How many times do we feel assaulted without any provocation or expectation? Isn't that just like the devil, to walk up to us as a familiar face and let us have it?

> *"Be of sober spirit, be on the alert. Your adversary, the devil, prowls around like a roaring lion, seeking someone to devour."*
>
> 1 Peter 5:8, NASB

NAP TIME

It's a paper cup filled with ... wait for it ... a latte and recovery and murky deep water.

Fatigue is not my friend.

It changes me. It hurts me. I lose hope and joy. I forget to be grateful.

The hamster wheel of life has no regard for health or a grateful perspective. Its constant turning compels us to run harder, faster, and longer in unending pursuit of things and stuff. Maybe we should take a break from the running and rest?

It is in the resting we recover and reset and remember who we are, and Whose we are, and the life we have been called to live.

> *"It is in vain that you rise up early and go late to rest, eating the bread of anxious toil; for he gives to his beloved sleep."*
>
> **Psalm 127:2, ESV**

MOVING OUT

It's "the Bucks of the Star" as the boys like to call it and limbo and deep water full of strangers.

Three of them showed up today. Strangers—sent in to pack up our household goods. They are efficient and professional. The men noticed and named all the players in the Big Red Machine picture. She asked how I was doing ...

Open door to the deep water. I'm beginning to understand why Jesus asked His followers to drop everything and follow Him. No delays. No wrapping up or packing up.

The wrapping up and packing up leave me in limbo. Painfully waiting for what's next. I am not fully here, and I'm not yet there. It's all but impossible to be fully anything for anyone when life is just waiting.

> *Jesus said, "Come, follow Me!"*
> **Matthew 4:19, NIV**

GET YOUR HEAD IN THE GAME

It's a keto coffee in the Snoopy Christmas mug and April snow (gotta love Michigan!) and black and white deep water.

Not everyone wins. In life, there is no gold medal for showing up. There is no trophy just because you participated.

The little's winning baseball team had a tough loss last night. One of those unexpected and inexplicable losses. No one likes to lose. Trust me when I say I understand that on a "whole 'nother level." I wasn't there, but I am sure the head coach had something to say to those boys about getting their heads back in the game and showing up to play.

The great thing is, that's where it ended. This morning is a new opportunity, and tonight is another game. It's a sport, so winning and losing are important, but ultimately, winning and learning is the better road. Rather than soaking in defeat, the boys have an opportunity to learn.

Kinda reminds me of the opportunity Jesus places in front of us. You can stick with your losses and wallow in your sadness and frustration, or you can learn the lesson and move on.

THE TIMES THEY ARE A-CHANGIN'

It's an almond milk latte in the totally worn and indistinguishable Miami Mom mug and a morning of motivation and long-term deep water.

Nine-plus years. 9+ YEARS. I never in my wildest imagination would have thought I'd be in this not-an-athlete season for this long. I mean, I get life is lived in seasons, but what the heck?!

I used to be an athlete. People. I was a serious athlete. It is WHAT I DID. And then it wasn't. And I've floundered. I've lived a lot of life in other ways and shapes and forms, but not as an athlete. No goals to meet. No struggles to overcome. At least not physically. Not as an athlete. I've missed that self, that identity, that purpose.

As I sat watching the Losing Sight of Shore documentary, I wondered again and again, "Why God? Why such a huge upheaval? Such an awesome redirect?" And then the deep water.

I was an athlete gifted by God but relying on my own strength. It's been 9+ years of living like Job. The very thing I used to form my identity had to be taken away in order for me to find my true, authentic identity in Him. I'm not sure what athletic endeavors may or will come my way, but I am sure of this—I will do it with a complete understanding of my strength and its source. I will do whatever comes next to glorify Him.

JUST NOT FEELIN' IT

It's an anticipated glass of something new and date night and not what I had hoped for deep water.

Today was going to be the day. This doctor was going to have THE answers. Until it wasn't. Until she didn't.

Gosh darn it, what do you do when what you hoped for, what you felt you really, truly needed, doesn't come to fruition? Where does your faith take you in "those" moments?

I hate waiting. The quiet thing is in process. I'm not asking to learn any more patience; thank you very much. I'm just not feeling this one …

And the deep water.

My hope isn't in a doctor. My hope isn't in a test. Yes, they can provide answers, treatments, and hopefully a plan, but let my hope be in Him. Then and only then will the lack of what I seek begin to settle into prayerful peace.

> *"Let all that I am wait quietly before God, for my hope is in Him."*
>
> **Psalm 62:5, NLT**

CUSTOM MADE ARMOR

It's espresso with cashew milk in the Jane mug and fighting through the pain and TGIF planning.

Was it life-changing, that thing Satan threw at you? Abuse? Disease? Divorce? Was it a temporary yet significant mountain? Job loss? Sports injury? Was it a seemingly un-winnable challenge? Healthy living? Sobriety?

Deep water truth: God's got you. Which means you've got this! Whatever "it" is, however long it lasts, however your life is redirected. Your armor is way better and your weapons way more potent than anything the devil can throw at you.

Just like the song says, "Hang on, help is on the way."

> *"I call upon You, for You will answer me, O God; incline Your ear to me; hear my words."*
>
> **Psalm 107:28, ESV**

A NOT-SO-HOSTILE TAKEOVER

It's an almond milk latte in the Seghesio mug and time with friends and making it to the top deep water.

The Bible has a lot to say about mountains—literal and figurative. Popular culture has a lot to say about overcoming hurdles. Quite a few songs have been sung about conquering that "thing" that keeps you stuck or knocks you down.

I am here to tell you ... There are mountains to climb, and hurdles to jump, and more things that will try and keep you where you are or knock you back a step or two than there are to push you on. That, my friends, is where faith takes over. It isn't where faith comes in or enters the picture. That moment, those mountains, are where faith takes over. Completely.

Today's deep water reminds me of how many literal mountains I've climbed. It inspires me to climb the figurative ones as well.

Onward and upward.

> *"The Sovereign Lord is my strength! He makes me as surefooted as a deer, able to tread upon the heights."*
>
> **Habakkuk 3:19, NLT**

UNDER PRESSURE

It's celebratory margaritas and six crates worth of reducing and this. This deep water.

"I'm just tired." "I'm just so stressed." "There's just so much going on right now. Can you even understand?!"

Jesus was beaten and scourged and hung on a cross, and not once did He speak harshly to His accusers and tormentors.

What you say when you're under pressure is about your internal truth. No excuses.

NO WAY OUT

It's the healthy mocha in the New Orleans mug and baseball sunburn and dogs blowing their coats.

It's amazing what you can do when you have no other choice. How strong you can be. The fortitude and determination.

It's the reason doctors and nutritionists and health coaches tell you to take everything you shouldn't eat out of the house. It's the reason people hire personal trainers. It's the reason people have accountability partners.

Whether a literal option or a mental shift, when we have no other choice, when we have no way out, we are left with moving forward in epic proportions.

THE MANTLE OF OPPRESSION

It's the healthy mocha in the pumpkin mug and layering up against the already negative temperatures and doing battle as a team.

I don't like being down for the count. Recovering from a surgery that was more involved than originally anticipated has been a struggle. Maybe it is in part the result of having MS, or maybe it is just what it is, but coming out of anesthesia has left me feeling foggy and fragile for days.

I don't like it.

I am not comfortable in the space where I am not entirely whole and able-bodied and quick-minded. I do not like the experience of being "less than." It isn't just that I don't like it. It's that it makes me feel bad about myself. The cloud of guilt and shame overwhelms me. It tells me that I am not allowed this time of rest and recovery.

When did it happen? When did I become entirely responsible for being perfect at all times and in all places? Another one of those great lies from the pit of hell. The deep water reminds me that the burden of being perfect isn't real. The need to be perfect is a falsehood not to be achieved. God's grace and mercy surround me and remind me that I am allowed to just be.

Whatever struggle you are facing today, I want to encourage you. You are allowed to just be. You do not have to be perfect. You do not have to do everything perfectly. Take off that mantle of oppression. Allow yourself space to be cared for. Rest in the truth that you are loved immeasurably.

> *"But He said to me, 'My grace is sufficient for you, for my power is made perfect in weakness.' Therefore I will boast all the more gladly about my weaknesses, so that Christ's power may rest on me."*
>
> **2 Corinthians 12:9, NIV**

THE DISCIPLINE OF PATIENCE

It's a healthy mocha in the chrysanthemum mug and Indian Matchmaker Season 2 and one last day of summer break.

It's amazing what you can learn if you keep your eyes and ears open. Little tidbits in the midst of seemingly vapid activity. Today, Auntie Sima from Mumbai taught me the Latin root of patience. And what a lesson!

Etymology. From Middle English pacience, from Old French pacience (modern French patience), from Latin patientia ("suffering; endurance, patience"), from patiens, present active participle of patior ("suffer, experience, wait"), ultimately from Proto-Indo-European *peh₁- ("to hurt").

Y'all! Patience comes from suffering! It comes from hurting. I'm sure I have had a superficial awareness of the truth of it, but to have it defined has opened the deep water floodgates.

Patience is a flower that grows in the midst of thorns. Patience is a lesson learned in the pool of sharks. Patience isn't just that skill we grasp over time—it is the skill gleaned from toil and blisters and cuts and scrapes. When we ask for patience, it is to understand we will undergo an attack of one kind or another on our own personal peace.

Whether it is a colicky baby or a painful medical procedure. An unruly teen or an ailing parent. A personal battle or a legal battle. Patience is the armor that grows like a stalactite, drip-by-drip, painful moments, and lifelong struggles.

Lest I forget, I am reminded that I am here. Today. I have learned and earned a goodly amount of patience. I can testify to the lyrics, "What doesn't kill you makes you stronger ..." I can testify to the blessing of a lesson in patience well learned.

> *"But let patience have her perfect work, that ye may be perfect and entire, wanting nothing."*
>
> **James 1:4, KJV**

BE OF GOOD CHEER

It's the Nespresso advent calendar sweet vanilla coffee in the naughty or nice mug and a good old-fashioned head cold and comfy clothes and hot toddies to make it all better.

What's the difference? What is the difference between being positive and hopeful and not complaining and being honest and allowing our burdens to be shared? How often in this social media-filtered, oh-so-perfect culture do we hide our less-than-perfect moments and seasons? How many times do we keep the hard truth of our struggles to ourselves, suffering in silence?

"But I don't want to be a burden."

"But others have it so much worse."

"But … but … but."

Whether it's a head cold or cancer. A broken bone or a broken marriage. You are not alone. I know you may think you are, feel you are, but you are not. The God of all creation sees you, and He knows your struggle, and He loves you more than you could ever dream or imagine. His promises are not to leave us or forsake us. Hold fast, dear one. There will be mountains and valleys, and in them, we are not alone.

I see you. Hang in there. At Christmastime, when so many seem so joyful, I see you. You can borrow my smile. I'll hold your hand … you are not alone.

Be of good cheer, my friend.

> *"Have I not commanded you? Be strong and courageous. Do not be afraid; do not be discouraged, for the Lord your God will be with you wherever you go."*
>
> **Joshua 1:9, NIV**

ROLLIN', ROLLIN', ROLLIN'

It's bottled water and blackout curtains and respite in the midst of the storm.

Change requires movement. Sometimes, moving means falling. Falling isn't failure. Falling is movement.

Keep on moving.

AUTHENTIC LIFE

An authentic life is one where we embrace both the beauty and the brokenness, finding healing in the most unexpected places. Restored and redeemed, we learn that the journey toward wholeness isn't about perfection, but about being true to who we are in Christ. In the depths of our struggles and triumphs, we open ourselves up to the power of vulnerability, the strength of grace, and the peace that comes from knowing we are fully seen, loved, and continually transformed.

DESTINY'S CHILD

What day is it???? It's game day baby!

The London Fog has come and gone, and the dogs have had their romp, and the deep water is, well, deep.

"I just want to find myself, my purpose, the thing for which God has destined me."

It sounds really good. It is most likely heartfelt. It may, however, miss the mark. When we focus on ourselves, the "me, myself, and I" of things, even when looking for God within us, we walk a very fine line. Be aware.

Look for Christ and you are certain to find yourself.

> *"Yes, everything else is worthless when compared with the infinite value of knowing Christ Jesus my Lord. For His sake, I have discarded everything else, counting it all as garbage, so that I could gain Christ."*
>
> **Philippians 3:8, NLT**

FLY TRAPS AND MOUSE TRAPS AND BEAR TRAPS, OH MY

It's French drinking chocolate and another scarf day and forward-looking deep water.

Sometimes I get stuck. The past can be a bit of an albatross. The things that trap me, more often than not, seem to have a common thread—the actions of others have damaged my soul. I am tied to the hurt—longstanding, life-altering hurt, and it moves within me like a horror film fog.

I'm doing a lot of work to recognize and put those negative experiences to bed. Give them a rest, and me too. I want to scream the names of the offenses, squash them into unrecognizable bits, and burn them into ashes. And then the deep water ...

When we focus on the negative, our perspective becomes just that—negative. I'm not saying to ignore painful life experiences or their impact on who we are and how we see and do life. But I am insisting that I no longer live in reaction to those hurts. My compass can no longer be centered on who did what and when and how it derailed my life.

Acknowledge the pain and then walk into gratitude. Find the space where being thankful trumps being hurt. If I hadn't experienced decades of abuse, I wouldn't be able to minister to others who share that story. If I hadn't been bullied mercilessly throughout junior high and high school, I wouldn't have the heart for the accused, the wounded, and those needing the most tender hearts and encouragement.

If I hadn't _____, I wouldn't be able to _____.

Where have you lived in pain and darkness? How has it changed you? Can you find the gratitude in those terrible, ugly places and let God use them for good?

> *"Be thankful in all circumstances, for this is God's will for you who belong to Christ Jesus."*
>
> **1 Thessalonians 5:18, NLT**

SHORT AND SWEET

It's a Mac-procured latte in a paper cup and time with my A-team and freedom-filled deep water.

Where do you hide? What do you hide? How does your blanket of shame distance you from loving others as yourself or, better yet, loving yourself?

It's the strong one who dares to cry. It's the strong one who humbles themselves enough to admit, "Me too."

Today, I think that one of the most profound statements in all of the Bible is also the shortest. "Jesus wept."

Vulnerability is strength. Jesus humbled Himself enough to become a man and live like us … and with us … and for us. He became vulnerable in ways we cannot even comprehend and, in doing so, showed us the utmost in love.

CAMERA READY

It's a long-finished Moscow Mule and fighting through the cribbage tournament with my mom and termination dust deep water.

There was a time when I wouldn't leave my home, dorm room, or apartment without full hair and makeup. My outward appearance was everything. My outward appearance and how I felt in presenting myself to the world mattered more than anything. My looks were my identity.

Fast forward 30+ years. Fast forward through the trauma and the abuse and everything social media has ever said about beauty. Fast forward to now. No makeup. No fancy, expensive hairstyle. Just me. Just the me that God rescued from the depths.

As the leaves fall from the trees and the snow descends upon the highest peaks, I am reminded that beauty is the most glorious in its pure, unadulterated self.

> *"Don't be concerned about the outward beatify of fancy hairstyles, expensive jewelry, or beautiful clothes. You should clothe yourselves with the beauty that comes from within, the unfading beauty of a gentle and quiet spirit, which is so precious to God."*
>
> 1 Peter 3:3-4, NLT

WHO, ME?

It's a salon mug filled with water and maintenance as self-care and most excellent recovery celebrations courtesy of The Prisoner.

For many seasons, I owned others' observations. I shrank from blessings in response to others' perceptions and jealous commentary. "Yes, but …" was my mantra. Negate the good. Mitigate the generosity of the Lord and reward for very hard work.

But.

But …

The Lord does not ask us to shrink from good. Dare I say, even great? The Lord blesses and rewards and requires, but humility is a long way from denying His goodness to make another feel better. No one knows, let alone understands, what battles have been fought and which wars have been won.

Today, the deep water reminds me to celebrate others' victories. To smile at their good and great and abundant. Today, I am reminded that everyone has fought battles about which I know nothing. The reward is theirs and does not negate mine.

OH, YES YOU CAN

It's a Mac-made mocha in the pretty Poland mug and getting ready to launch and new blue layers because Alaska in the spring is pretty chilly.

Want some seriously deep water?

You don't have to stay where you are. You have the ability to change. To move.

Maybe moving doesn't look like leaving. Maybe moving doesn't look like a crazy, drastic upheaval. Maybe moving looks like one small step in another direction. And then another small step. And then …

You, my friend, do not need to uproot yourself to move but never forget: you can move. You are not a tree.

IN SICKNESS AND IN HEALTH

It's espresso with coconut sugar and heavy cream in the William & Mary mug and hints of autumnal cool and the love of neighbors.

It's been a difficult season, this being sick and not having answers. Lots of doctors, lots of needles, lots of isolation. Pain has caused me to withdraw. Hugs are more than I can tolerate. And I don't have my people. Or so I thought.

Today's deep water brings freedom. I am not the athlete. I am not the strong one. I am not the abuse survivor. I am not _____, and my new friends, my neighbors, have rallied around me. They are not expecting me to be anything more than what I am. They are loving me, caring for me. They lift me with their prayers. They offer their help. The burden of being what I once was is lifted as they surround me just as I am.

The marriage vows of "in sickness and in health" don't apply just to marriage. They apply to friendship as well. Being loved and valued for the "remains of who we are" is an amazing gift.

> *"Bear one another's burdens, and so fulfill the law of Christ."*
>
> **Galatians 6:2, ESV**

LIFE AND DEATH

It's an afternoon pumpkin spice latte in the Seghesio mug and broken back recovery and black on black on black because sometimes creativity is just too much.

What is the promise of autumn?

In short, the deep water reminds me that this season of beautiful death promises a new spring. Even beautiful things must end. Sleep must occur before one can awake.

Pause to reflect on the promise of endings that allow for new beginnings.

THAT DOG WON'T HUNT

It's an Italian blend in the pinot glasses and goodbye to the Texas license and stuffing it deep water.

"It's not that big of a deal."

"Nah. I don't really need to talk about it."

"If I just don't think about it, it'll be okay."

How often do we suppress and repress the things (actions, words) that cause us pain? How often do we simply pretend the hurt isn't real or the situation isn't as difficult as it feels? All too often, we choose to stuff the pain, the fear, and the disappointment somewhere deep inside instead of confronting the monster (however big or small) head-on.

Ladies and gentlemen, I'm here to tell you "that dog won't hunt."

> *"I've told you about hungry dogs in the cellar... If you don't feed them and don't acknowledge them, at some point, they are going to get out somehow and do something unsavory."*
>
> **Norman R. Augustine**

Deal with it, or it will come back to bite you in the ...

DISASTER RELIEF

It's coffee with half-and-half in the Miami mug and having the difficult conversations and when will it be autumn?!?! Oh the waiting.

Let's be real. My kitchen is always clean, and my bed is always made. Not lying. Until last night.

An utter disaster, my friends, is what greeted me this morning, and this is where the deep water met me.

Sometimes it's okay. Just to be okay. No spit. No polish. We all want to present our best selves. What about presenting our not-so-best selves? God doesn't mind. He even welcomes our not-so-best. He lives with us there. Holds us there. Until.

And when "until" arrives, we can move on and return to our best.

> *"My grace is all you need. My power works best in weakness."*
>
> **2 Corinthians 12:9, NLT**

I'M ALRIGHT. DON'T NOBODY WORRY 'BOUT ME.

It's an almond milk latte in the Berlin mug and sunshine and quiet.

Today's deep water is pretty straightforward.

"Will I be okay?" she asked.

"If you choose to be, you will," he offered.

> *"I have set before you life and death, blessings and curses. Now choose life, so that you and your children may live."*
>
> **Deuteronomy 30:19, NIV**

So often, we keep ourselves in bondage. We choose death. It really is just that. Either we choose such that we walk toward life, or we choose to walk in death. Personally. Relationally. In thought, word, deed. God recognizes the unending struggle of life and death. And He offers us the path toward life. We need only choose.

Yeah, yeah. I know. "We need only choose," you say. It's not that easy. God knows that as well. He left us the Holy Spirit to live with us and in us for that very reason. He loves us enough to give us every tool we need to choose life. Reach out. Grab life. Crawl on your hands and knees. Touch life. Choose life.

YOU CAN'T SEE ME

It's a second cup of espresso with half-and-half and reno prep and culling the herd closet and armoire exercises.

You can see it. The absence of joy. If you look beyond the pretty family picture, you can see the distance, the absence in her eyes. You have to look. You must be aware.

He is extremely happy. The daughter has completed something worth capturing, and she is equally excited. The wife (mother), however, looks beyond the camera. Her eyes are blank. Her smile is too small compared to the others in the photo.

I wonder where she has gone. How is it we can pretend well enough to go unnoticed? I want to tell her I see. I see her and the lack of joy. I see her.

So does God. I want to let her know she is not alone. So does He. He never leaves us all alone.

Smile, dear one. You are seen.

> *"So she called the name of the Lord who spoke to her, 'You are a God of seeing,' for she said, 'Truly here I have seen Him who looks after me.'"*
>
> **Genesis 16:13, ESV**

HERE TODAY. GONE TOMORROW.

It's another hazelnut coffee with half-and-half in the pumpkin mug and time for rest and seasonal deep water.

Autumn is, by far, my most favorite season. It ushers in the cold temperatures that soothe my soul and the dark mornings that beckon the fireplace and a cup of something warm. Autumn is an opportunity for letting go and the hope of a clean slate that a hard freeze and white snow promise.

As I wandered the back garden with the pups this morning, drinking in all the beauty it afforded, the deep water reminded me. One of the things that makes autumn so precious is its very nature. Autumn is fleeting. Here one day. Gone the next. It forces us to slow down just long enough to glimpse all it holds before it rushes off. Autumn bursts on the scenes in grandeur. A grandeur that's not meant to be forever. It reminds us to slow down, if only for a brief moment. To savor time. To appreciate what will come … and go … and leave us longing for more.

This morning, I am reminded that Jesus did much the same thing. He burst onto the scene to show us all that was beautiful and hopeful and full of promise. He gave us a glimpse of the opportunity to be cleaned and made new, much like the white of the winter snow. And, just like that, He was gone. With a promise to return and bring us all that we could ever dream or hope for.

> *"In a little while, you won't see Me anymore. But a little while after that, you will see Me again."*
>
> **John 16:16, NLT**

PRETTY IN PINK

It's fuzzy pink bubbles of Iron Horse spring cuvée in a favorite Italian flute and open windows and peonies peonies everywhere.

There was a season in my life where I didn't wear pink. Where I didn't appreciate pink flowers or enjoy pink bubbles. To me, pink represented innocence and beauty, and for a season, that was lost to me.

The beautiful peonies and the lovely bubbles are a deep water reminder that God can heal all wounds and make all things beautiful. What have you put aside because it brings back bad memories? What beauty are you missing because evil has robbed you?

Enjoy the pink.

"He has made everything beautiful in its time…"
Ecclesiastes 3;11, NKJV

ONE, TWO, BUCKLE MY SHOE

It's a Mac-made latte in the Seghesio mug and a big dog party and snow flurries for the snowboarder among us.

For most of my life, I thought I had to be last. I believed a "good Christian" would never, ever put themselves before anyone else. In fact, a "good Christian" would never even consider themselves, lest they be self-centered, which Jesus most certainly was not.

Until the deep water.

First, love God. Then, love others as you love yourself. Umm … Love yourself???

We can only give out of the abundance from within. Not only is self-care not selfish, it is the very basis for loving others. Love yourself well = love others well.

Love God first. Love yourself next. Then, love others out of the overflow of love within you.

COMFORTABLY NUMB

It's ice water (why???) in the cherry blossom tumbler and 35 degrees to start this Alaskan spring day and searching for the motivation.

In theory, numbing pain can and does help heal. Doctors employ a variety of pain relievers to assist in healthy, specific and localized repair and recovery. For a moment in time, numbing pain is a good thing. The deep water urges caution when numbing pain, however.

Emotional pain isn't healed by numbing it. Quite the opposite. Emotional pain needs to be felt. Considered. Addressed. When we numb our emotions, we numb all of them, and it is the positive emotions that are key to healing the painful ones.

Feel all the feels.

> *"And after you have suffered a little while, the God of all grace, who has called you to His eternal glory in Christ, will Himself restore, confirm, strengthen, and establish you."*
>
> **1 Peter 5:10, ESV**

SETTLING IN

It's the routine mocha in the happy place mug and early morning quiet and an indoor kind of day.

Two weeks of travel has left me worn. Not worn out but worn. Time to hit pause for a moment.

Today, amidst the chill and rain, I will clean. Bake. Organize. These tasks calm me. Fill me. A settled space equals a settled me. I offer up the work of my hands for God's peace. Grateful for His provision.

Today, take a moment. Listen to the ebb and flow of life around you. Settle into the task at hand. Seek the deep water.

"A heart at peace gives life to the body ..."
Proverbs 14:30, NIV

FEED ME!

It's a sparkling water in a green bottle and waiting in the car line and Groundhog Day. Again.

What do you do when you're angry? What do you do when you're sad? What do you do when you're happy? What do you do when you're frustrated? What do you do when you're celebrating? What do you do when you're lonely?

Me? I feed the feelings.

Self-motivation and self-control go by the wayside. All the work, and all the learning, and all the know-how mean nothing when all of the feelings are there. Why is that?

Why are feelings such dictators? It is the proverbial tail wagging the dog. And I, for one, am just tired of it. Deep water to the rescue…

> *"The heart is deceitful above all things, and desperately sick; who can understand it?"*
>
> **Jeremiah 17:9, ESV**

Here, perhaps a better word would be feelings. Heart = feelings. The Bible talks about taking every thought captive. It also talks about being aware of, even wary of, our feelings. Don't be surprised that feelings want to push you around.

Grace recognizes the kind of bully your feelings can and will be. Grace tells you that you are not alone. Grace tells you that you are not condemned when your feelings sidetrack you.

Here's to feeding the truth.

SORT OF, KIND OF, MAYBE

It's the healthy mocha in the pumpkin mug and day two of after-travel reset and early morning doggo snuggles.

I've been hiding. Trying to cover up the not-so-comfortable bits. And for a time, it has worked. Sort of.

My team, my people, soft toss the deep water my way. Encouraging and honest. Hopeful and true.

Hiding is not healthy.

Whatever you hide, you don't heal. Mental, emotional, physical, or spiritual. It really doesn't matter. The dark doesn't discriminate.

Today, I'm uncovering. Bringing the not comfortable to the light. Seeing what that feels like.

Today looks like coming out of hiding.

> *"But if we are living in the light, as God is in the light, then we have fellowship with each other, and the blood of Jesus, His Son, cleanses us from all sin."*
>
> **1 John 1:7, NLT**

IN PURSUIT OF HOPE

It's a plain ol' water in the pink Stanley and the rust puffer vest to balance the season and on-our-knees discernment.

You're never going to create the life you want by trying to fix the life you don't want.

Deep water truth. Running from something you don't want is based in fear. Running toward something you do want is based in hope.

Fear is finite. Hope is infinite.

Fear cannot live where hope exists.

> *"Let us hold fast the confession of our hope without wavering, for He who promised is faithful."*
>
> **Hebrews 10:23, ESV**

PLAYING FOR THE AUDIENCE

It's a Kofenya oat milk latte in a paper cup and outgrowing youth eyeglasses and "I couldn't have said it better myself" deep water.

Be who you are. All the time. Different people don't require a different you. I've never understood the playing for an audience change of personality.

God made you to, well, be you.

> "Before I formed you in the womb, I knew you, and before you were born, I consecrated you ..."
>
> **Jeremiah 1:5, ESV**

VOICE AMPLIFICATION

It's an almond milk latte and snuggly puppies and understanding-filled deep water.

"Jackie, you live out loud. And that's a good thing."

My beloved counselor tried to get me to see how not hiding was a good thing, but it didn't feel good. I felt, still feel, vulnerable. Living out loud leaves you very exposed.

Why? I wonder time and again. I ask God what purpose there might be in "living out loud." And He is so wonderful to make connecting with others part of this out-loudness.

The connection that comes when you literally feel another's feelings is about as close as one can get. I see you. I feel your feelings. I can see you, even when you can't see yourself. It's such a gift for me, me in ministry.

Now I understand part of living out loud is to help me as well. How awesome is that?!

> *"I will give thanks to You because I have been so amazingly and miraculously made. Your works are miraculous, and my soul is fully aware of this."*
>
> **Psalm 139:14, GW**

LOUD PIPES SAVE LIVES

It's an almond milk latte in the Miami Mom mug and more muddy paws and middle-of-the-night deep water.

"Loud pipes save lives." I sat up in bed wondering. Okay, God, what do You want to tell me about motorcycles?

"Loud pipes save lives."

Yep. Tell me, please, there is sleeping to be done.

Motorcycles aren't afraid to be motorcycles. In fact, their "loudness" offers them protection. "Loud pipes save lives." Their "loudness" can save them. Perhaps save others?

Oh, the deep water ... Being bold in our faith (whatever that looks like for each of us) can save us. Perhaps save others.

Ride on.

> "... that utterance may be given to me, that I may open my mouth boldly to make known the mystery of the gospel, for which I am an ambassador in chains; that in it I may speak boldly as I ought to speak."
>
> **Ephesians 6:19-20, NKJV**

GAINING PERSPECTIVE

Growing up is a journey of deepening our faith and learning to see the world through God's eyes, adjusting our perspective as we encounter life's challenges. The deep waters of struggle and uncertainty often call us closer to Him, inviting us to trust in His plan and grace. By embracing His guidance and shifting our perspective, we come to realize that what once seemed overwhelming can be a path to spiritual maturity and greater understanding of His love.

I CAN SEE CLEARLY NOW

It's a glass of something bubbly and pink and no layers whatsoever and hearing the whales deep water.

What side of the clouds are you on?

The reality is that there will always be clouds. Sunny days. Rainy days. Perhaps even a long stretch in between, but there will always be clouds.

The deep water reminds me that it's all about perspective. On one side of the clouds is sunshine and breezes and relaxation. On the other side of the clouds is torment and hunkering down and hiding. One side is freedom, and the other side is a storm.

It's all about perspective.

> *"As we look not to the things that are seen but to the things that are unseen. For the things that are seen are transient, but the things that are unseen are eternal."*
>
> **2 Corinthians 4:18, ESV**

GERANIMO!

It's a cardamom latte courtesy of the Mac and air conditioning and learning.

How many times have we looked at another struggling to be or do what we want? How many times have we lost our peace being frustrated because someone else "just doesn't get it"? Better yet, how many times have we been impatient or less than gentle or even unkind because another hasn't been the person or acted the way we wanted?

My spiritual mentor shared something that presented an a-ha moment this morning. One of those "Oh, I've been that person" lessons.

> "Becoming upset and impatient over the failings of someone is like responding to his falling into a ditch by throwing oneself in another."
>
> **St. Bonaventure**

PLUG YOUR EARS

Between the thunderstorms earlier and the fireworks this evening the dogs are about as neurotic as ever and then the deep water...

What is the loud noise in your life? The noise that is absolutely terrifying you? Can you shift your perception and hear it from a different angle?

The thunder comes with much-needed rain and cooler temperatures. The fireworks are entertaining, a light extravaganza.

So often, what we see, hear, think, or feel as terrifying may not be so. Maybe, just maybe, it's the perspective that's in need of a change?

The dogs and I, we're huddled up, waiting it out. They can't quite grasp how wonderful the storm and fireworks are. Maybe we can huddle up with God and wait out whatever we're terrified by, too.

OH, YES, I CAN

It's coffee with cream in the plain white mug and wishing for the winter robe and impatient deep water.

It's chilly this morning. The not-so-little middle, aka fire maker, is still sleeping, and the firewood has yet to be brought in. I'm impatient. I mumble, pleading for him to wake up and make me a fire. He sleeps on … and then the deep water.

"You are capable."

That's it.

Yes, I can make the fire. But it's so lovely when someone makes the fire for me. And I'm snuggled up in the soft wool blanket.

"You are capable."

But … too often we wait, shivering, for someone else to make us feel all warm and cuddly when we are capable—more than capable—of building the fire ourselves. God equips us. It's up to us to move beyond comfort into action.

You are capable. Now, what are you going to do???

> *"I can do all this through Him who gives me strength."*
> **Philippians 4:13, NIV**

RULES, SCHMULES

Well shoot. I thought I was gliding into late afternoon and a time of relaxation and then I began watching my latest recommended TED talk.

This is a season of paradigm shifts in my life. These truths are running me over, and sitting me down, and making me reconsider the majority of the lenses through which I have and do see life.

> *"A wise person knows when and how to make 'the exception to every rule.'"*
>
> **Barry Schwartz**

Dang it. Dagnabbit. This rule follower (yes, yours truly) has been holding a flame to the Mac's feet for 29+ years about bending the rules. New lens. Full sincerity. He is super wise. I have been short-sighted.

So glad God saw enough of me to put me with this man.

TURN AROUND, BRIGHT EYES

The milkadamia latte is long gone and the snow has fallen melted fallen melted frozen melted and frozen again and the deep water caught my gaze this afternoon.

After a week of sitting at my desk writing, I finally ventured out today. As we drove out, the sun shone brightly overhead, and the mountains heralded God's majesty. We remarked on the awesome beauty that surrounds us.

As we turned back toward home, the sky was dark and sullen. It was a marked change from only 30 minutes earlier. And, just like that, the deep water.

Turn back 180 degrees and the sun was still shining and the mountains just as glorious. Only our direction changed. I wonder how often we settle on the more somber of views, the more sullen of views when the light is right there if we'd only turn and look.

> *"If you look for Me wholeheartedly, you will find Me."*
> **Jeremiah 29:13, NLT**

THE LAW OF INERTIA

It's a healthy mocha in the pretty Poland mug and—still—the pink winter robe and planning for the future.

Perspective is reality.

Jump in the deep water with me.

Not so long ago, I would have said being able to see your breath when you let the dogs out in the morning means it is cold outside. That was my perspective.

This morning, I opened the back door to let the dogs out and thought, "It's warm today." And then I saw my breath swirl up into the light sky. Hmm.

Is it cold? Warm? Is it right? Wrong? Is it good? Bad? Have I so acclimated to the Alaska-level cold that "regular" Ohio-level cold is no longer cold?

Perspective influences everything. Let's make sure we keep our perspective in check and be open to seeing things from another angle.

Reality isn't always as immovable as we'd like to believe.

> *"Oh, the depth of the riches and wisdom and knowledge of God! How unsearchable are His judgments and how inscrutable His ways!"*
>
> **Romans 11:33, ESV**

THE TIDE IS HIGH

It's the healthy mocha in the blue Ikea glass and new things in the midst of waiting for the rest of the things and grassy dew-covered feet.

How do you find the gratitude in the midst of crazy? Once you find it, how do you hold on to it?

A new puppy = grateful. The corresponding lack of sleep = not-so-grateful. Doug the dog discovering he has a new friend = grateful. Bella being a grumpy gal over the new puppy = not-so-grateful. The new puppy very quickly learning potty training = grateful. Bella getting into the garbage in the night and getting sick and crying until I understand she needs to be let out = not-so-grateful. This dance of gratitude and struggle goes on and on ...

And then the deep water.

This ebb and flow is the tide of life. To hope for consistency is to erase the mountain peaks. To wish away the valleys is to diminish the lessons learned and overlook the opportunities.

Today, I will be grateful that I can take a power nap after a mostly sleepless night. I will focus on the blessing rather than curse the struggle. Today, I will be gentle with myself and others because it is more than okay to be still when I can.

"Let the peace of Christ rule in your hearts ..."
Colossians 3:15, NIV

OH, WOE IS ME

It's the healthy mocha in the snowman mug and the pretty pink winter robe and a soft pink sunrise to start the day.

It's no secret—I'm not a fan of the grey, rainy, chilly Ohio winters. Give me Alaska any day. It would be oh-so-easy to settle into the Eeyore-like humdrum this weather inspires. Enter the deep water …

Find the beauty.

I am an inherent optimist. It catches me off guard when I find myself in a space that is less than that. When the world around me seems dark and gloomy and absent beauty. As I enjoyed my coffee this morning, the Christmas tree lights came on to illuminate the darkness. The Mac knows how much I enjoy my gentle start to the morning and, every year, orchestrates the beauty and the light of the Christmas season to encourage me and surround me in the hope this season holds. As I sat in the still darkness of this day, the deep water encouraged me. "Find the beauty."

I'm hoping that in the midst of whatever busy season you are in and less than beautiful circumstances, and all the other things that can rob us of our joy, you will have a moment where you can see the beauty. Find the beauty.

> *"And now, dear brothers and sisters, one final thing. Fix your thoughts on what is true, and honorable, and right, and pure, and lovely, and admirable. Think about things that are excellent and worthy of praise."*
>
> **Philippians 4:8, NLT**

CHOOSING THE NARRATIVE

It's a nutty Irishman latte in a paper cup and crisp blue autumn and made-up deep water.

Life can be, well, dull. Routine becomes empty. Trusted and reliable … and boring. This is the stuff divorce and affairs are made of.

The deep water calls us to make some changes—in our perspective. Get your mind right, and the rest will follow. Tell yourself how great you have it. Create the story you need to realize what you have is ALL THAT.

> *"For as he thinks in his heart, so is he …"*
> **Proverbs 23:7, NKJV**

ONE LAST THOUGHT

The deep water is not reserved for a few special chosen people; it's open and available to all. Will we stay in the safety of the shallows, where life feels manageable and predictable, or venture deeper, where God's presence is more profound, albeit mysterious, and transformative. The invitation to explore is not reckless, but protected in the safety of the One who calls us there. The invitation is simple: come deeper *if you will*.

RISK IT FOR THE BISCUIT

It's the bedside table water in the DC cherry blossom Tervis and seven more minutes of daylight every single day and waiting for the Mac's return.

Here is one last thought for you: you get to choose.

There aren't any rules or hidden agendas. No barriers or bars. No puppet strings or boxes to check.

The deep water is open. Free. Possible.

Choosing and taking chances can feel too big—like it is too much responsibility. Too risky.

But choosing and taking chances is also the only way forward. You really do have to "risk it for the biscuit." And, oh, what a wonderful life lies ahead for you! The deep water awaits where you can discover richness beyond understanding and a joy that isn't dependent on circumstances.

Dive in.

PRAISE FOR DEEP WATER

As a Naval Aviator, I was trained to look for patterns, follow procedures, and stay calm under pressure. You don't just memorize everything—you carry a NATOPS Pocket Checklist. It lives in your flight suit and in the aircraft. It guides routine operations like engine start-ups and shutdowns, but more importantly, it's what you reach for in an emergency—when the lights are blinking, the smoke is thick, and every second counts.

Jackie's *Deep Water* reminds me of that checklist. It's tabbed by theme, grounded in Scripture, and designed to be used, whether you're easing into a quiet morning or trying to steady yourself mid-crisis. It doesn't waste time on fluff. It's real, relatable, and quietly effective.

Look, some might say this is technically a "chick book," but that doesn't mean men won't benefit from it. I plan to make sure a few of them do. In a world where many are spiritually flying blind, this book offers steady instrumentation. Read it once, then keep it close.

—*Captain Steve Malloy, US Navy (Retired)*

Deep Water is beautifully written and thoughtfully presented. It's the perfect blend of approachable, everyday storytelling and deep, thought-provoking reflection. Throughout these pages, themes of faith and family quietly anchor every chapter. Poignant, funny (Doug the dog's antics are so cute!), relatable, honest, and challenging—this book meets you right where you are and invites you deeper. It would make a meaningful gift for any season of life—from newlyweds to empty nesters. I plan to keep my copy on my bedside table to revisit again and again. Thank you for writing this, Jackie.

—*Jen Vallo*

Deep Water is a quiet, grace-filled invitation to dwell with God in the sacred stillness beneath the surface of everyday life. With the tender clarity of St. Thérèse, Jackie McCown shows us that the deepest truths are often found in small moments, quiet rituals, and honest questions. This is a book about presence over performance, trust over fear—a gentle current of hope flowing through the ordinary.

—Ryan Stambaugh

Jackie's words resonate, inspire, and challenge. She shares what are sometimes inconvenient and often uncomfortable truths she has discovered in relatable, day-to-day moments. She describes course-correction, beautifully illustrated by what we are instructed to do in Scripture. Her quiet voice makes it safe to try this on for ourselves.

Deep Water finds profound truth in the quiet of everyday, celebrates grace, and gives peace like a river.

—Mary Hoover

A friend in your back pocket—or a loving kick in the pants when you need something a little extra. Jackie's newest book is filled with the same kindness and wisdom that I have found in some of my most intimate moments of prayer. Her honest and thoughtful reflections tug at the ordinary and very real questions and struggles we encounter in everyday life, and offer encouragement, accompaniment, and hope for the future. Let yourself be loved through her words. You are worth it.

—Sammi Scolfaro

Deep Water is an immersion into the unmistakable voice and vision of Jackie, a friend whose words I've seen grow from social media posts into this beautifully crafted collection. I've had the privilege of walking alongside this project from edits to layout to publishing, and in every step, I've been struck by how uniquely she sees the world. Her writing carries a rare blend of honesty, depth, and tenderness, offering readers the gift of seeing the sacred in the everyday. In these pages, you'll find a voice like no other—steady, refreshing, and alive with the presence of God.

—Wendy K. Walters

ABOUT THE AUTHOR

Before she was a writer or speaker, Jackie was a wife navigating a public life behind the scenes and a mom raising three boys across 33 moves, cultures, and seasons—all while learning to find God not just in sanctuaries, but in school pickup lines and late-night prayers. Her journey through Calvinism, Anglicanism, and Catholicism has shaped a faith both deep and wide, rooted in grace and wonder. Today, she writes and speaks to create spaces of welcome—where faith feels like a shared table and the sacred is found in the everyday.

jackiemccown.com

www.ingramcontent.com/pod-product-compliance
Lightning Source LLC
Chambersburg PA
CBHW071233070526
44583CB00017B/2167